For Jimmy O, who loved and served the King.

Bob

*To my loving family and my family in Christ: you have prayed,
encouraged and sustained me in so many ways through this marathon.
And to my team at The Good Book Company, especially André and Alison:
I couldn't have done this without any of you!*

"For when I am weak, then I am strong."
(2 Corinthians 12 v 10)

Catalina

The Kingdom and the King Storybook Bible
© Bob Hartman, 2025

Published by The Good Book Company

thegoodbook.com | thegoodbook.co.uk | thegoodbook.com.au | thegoodbook.co.nz

Bob Hartman has asserted his right under the Copyright, Designs and Patents Act 1988 to be identified as author of this work.

Catalina Echeverri has asserted her right under the Copyright, Designs and Patents Act 1988 to be identified as illustrator of this work.

A CIP catalogue record for this book is available from the British Library.

Edited by Alison Mitchell | Illustrations by Catalina Echeverri | Design and art direction by André Parker

ISBN: 9781802543384 | JOB-008138 | Printed in China

CONTENTS

THE OLD TESTAMENT

1. The Creator King — 12
   Genesis 1 v 1 – 2 v 3

2. The First Rebellion — 16
   Genesis 3

3. The Ark and the Rainbow — 18
   Genesis 6 v 1 – 9 v 17

4. The Too-Tall Tower — 20
   Genesis 11 v 1-9

5. The King Makes a Nation — 22
   Genesis 12 v 1-9; 15 v 1-6; 17 v 1-16; 18 v 1-15; 21 v 1-7

6. The Nation Grows — 24
   Genesis 22 v 1-19; 24; 25 v 19 – 26 v 5; 27 – 33

7. The Nation Moves! — 26
   Genesis 37; 39 – 47

8. A Bulrush Basket and a Burning Bush — 28
   Exodus 1 v 1 – 4 v 16

9. King versus King — 30
   Exodus 5 – 10

10. The Redeemer King — 32
    Exodus 11 – 12

11. The Triumph of the King — 34
    Exodus 13 v 17 – 15 v 3

12. Another Kingly Covenant — 36
    Exodus 15 v 22 – 17 v 7; 19 – 24

13. Rebellion in the Wilderness — 38
    Exodus 24 v 12 – 32 v 35; Numbers 14 v 1-38

14. The King Who Takes Care of His People — 40
    Joshua 1 – 6

15. The King and His Judges — 42
    Judges 2 – 4; 6 – 7; 13 – 16; 1 Samuel 3 – 7

16. We Want a King! — 44
    1 Samuel 8

17. The People's King — 46
    1 Samuel 9 – 11; 13 v 1 – 14 v 23; 15

18. A King After God's Own Heart — 48
    1 Samuel 16 v 1-13

19. A Victory for God's King — 50
    1 Samuel 16 v 14 – 17 v 54

20. A Kingly Covenant with David — 54
    1 Samuel 18 v 6-16; 2 Samuel 7

21. A Wise King and a Kingdom Divided — 56
    1 Kings 3 v 1-28; 4 v 20 – 12 v 24

22. The True God — 58
    1 Kings 16 v 29 – 17 v 1; 18 v 17-39

23. One Kingdom Falls — 61
2 Kings 17 v 1-24; Hosea 1 v 2; 11 v 1-7

24. A Faithful King — 62
2 Kings 18 – 19

25. Pictures of the Coming King — 64
Taken from Isaiah

26. The Repentant King — 66
2 Chronicles 33 v 1-20

27. The King Who Found a Book — 68
2 Chronicles 34 – 35

28. Another Kingdom Falls — 70
Taken from Jeremiah

29. A Nation in Exile — 72
Daniel 1; 3; 6 – 7

30. A Remnant Returns — 74
*Ezra 1 – 7; Nehemiah 1 – 9;
Zechariah 9 v 9; Malachi 4 v 5-6*

THE NEW TESTAMENT

31. A King, at Last! — 78
Luke 1 v 5-25, 57-80

32. The Big Announcement! — 80
Luke 1 v 26-56; Matthew 1 v 18-25

33. A Sudden Angel Surprise — 82
Luke 2 v 1-20

34. The News Spreads — 84
Matthew 2 v 1-15

35. Two Temple Stories — 88
Luke 2 v 22-35, 41-52

36. The Herald of the King — 90
*Matthew 3 v 1-17; Mark 1 v 1-11;
Luke 3 v 1-22*

37. "If You Are the King..." — 92
Luke 4 v 1-13

38. The King Who Heals — 95
Matthew 4 v 23-25; Revelation 21 v 1-5

39. Home-Town Boy — 96
Luke 4 v 14-30

40. Disciples of the King — 98
Luke 5 v 1-11; John 1 v 43-51

41. Jesus, King of Creation — 101
Luke 8 v 22-25

42. Jesus, King of the Sabbath — 102
Matthew 12 v 1-14

43. Jesus, King of All — 104
Matthew 8 v 5-13

44. Jesus, the King Who Conquers Evil Spirits — 106
Luke 11 v 14-22

45. A Kingdom of Kids and Camels — 108
Luke 18 v 15-27

46. A Kingdom of Second (and Many More!) Chances — 110
Matthew 18 v 21-35

47. A Kingdom of Servants — 113
Mark 10 v 35-45

48. A Kingdom of the Lost and Found — 114
Luke 15 v 1-32

49. A Kingdom of Edges and Hedges — 116
Luke 14 v 12-24

50. A Kingdom of Unlikely Neighbours — 118
Luke 10 v 25-37

51. Pictures of the Kingdom — 120
Matthew 5 v 1-48

52. More Kingdom Pictures — 122
Matthew 6 v 1 – 7 v 27

53. The King on the Donkey — 124
Matthew 21 v 1-11; Luke 19 v 28-40

54. A King in Conflict — 126
Matthew 21 v 12-13; 24 v 1-2; 23 v 1-36; 26 v 14-16

55. The King's Supper — 130
Luke 22 v 7-23, 39-46

56. The King on Trial — 132
John 18 v 1 – 19 v 16

57. The King Is Dead — 134
Mark 15 v 16-47

58. Long Live the King! A Mysterious Shock — 136
Luke 24 v 1-12

59. Long Live the King!
    A Very Long Walk   138
    Luke 24 v 13-35

60. Long Live the King! The Door
    Was Locked   140
    Luke 24 v 36-49

61. The King Ascends   142
    Luke 24 v 50-53; Acts 1 v 6-11

62. The Holy Spirit Comes   144
    Acts 2 v 1-41

63. Bringing the Kingdom to Life 146
    Acts 2 v 42-47

64. The Beautiful Gate   148
    Acts 3 v 1 – 4 v 22

65. Saul Sees the King   150
    Acts 7 v 54 – 8 v 3; 9 v 1-19

66. An Ethiopian Follows the King 154
    Acts 8 v 4-8, 26-39

67. Cornelius, the Roman Centurion 156
    Acts 10 v 1-48

68. All About Paul   158
    Acts 9 v 20-31; 13 v 1-52; 17 v 16-34; Philippians 2 v 5-11

69. Visions of the King   160
    Revelation 1 v 9-20

70. New Heaven, New Earth!   162
    Revelation 21 – 22

WELCOME

You meet plenty of kings and queens when you read the Bible. Some of them were good; some were okay; and some were very, very bad. But none of them ruled over everything – and none of them ruled for ever.

None of them, in other words, were like God – the awesome, eternal, loving God who we meet on the very first page of the Bible and on every other page too. As we read about him creating our world, we discover that God is the real King. He rules over everyone and everything.

God the King made a perfect universe, with a perfect world for the first people to live in, where he ruled as King. But that first family, Adam and Eve, turned away from God. They wanted to rule their own lives instead of living with him as their King. From then on, God's perfect world was spoiled, and everyone turned their backs on him.

Wonderfully, from that moment on, even while people were busy turning away from him, God began to make amazing promises to send his people a new King. He would be a rescuing King whose kingdom would last for ever.

The rest of the Bible is about how God kept that special promise. In the Old Testament, there are lots of clues about who it would be and how he would come. And then – at the very first Christmas – the promised King arrived. He was Jesus Christ, born in the royal town of Bethlehem.

The New Testament part of the Bible tells us about Jesus' life and his teaching and the miracles he did that showed he was indeed the promised King. It also tells us that his enemies had him killed, but his Father, God, brought him wonderfully back to life, and how his friends watched Jesus disappear up into the sky when he went back to be with his Father in heaven. And all the while, Jesus grew his kingdom – starting with twelve followers, and then expanding to reach so many people that it soon became impossible to count them all.

In this storybook Bible, you'll trace the story of that kingdom and that King. Each story is carefully told to be true to the words in the Bible. If you also want to read the story for yourself in the Bible, that's great! You will find the Bible references (the parts of the Bible you need to read) under each chapter title. These are the main passages a story is based on, though there may be extra details that come from other passages as well.

We hope that this storybook Bible will help you get to know the King more and more, and to be excited about living in his kingdom – not just now but for ever.

1. THE CREATOR KING
GENESIS 1 v 1 – 2 v 3

In the beginning, there was God, the King.

But there were no people, nor any place for them to live.

So the King created that place – the heavens and the earth.

The earth was covered with darkness.

So, with a Breath and a Word, the King spoke. And there was light!

   Waters covered the earth – there was no shape to things, no order.

     So, with a Breath and a Word, he spoke. And between the waters above and the waters below, he made a safe place.

     Land! The King's people would need land beneath their feet.

     So, with a Breath and a Word, he spoke. And the waters gathered into seas and left behind mountains and plains and hills.

   Food! The King's people would need food.

So, with a Breath and a Word, he spoke. And grain flowed through fields, and trees filled with fruit.

The King's people would need a way to tell the time and to mark the seasons.

So, with a Breath and a Word, he spoke. And, up in the heavens, they appeared: a big light for the day; a smaller light for the night; and little lights twinkling far beyond.

The waters were empty.

So, with a Breath and a Word, God spoke. And life, large and small and strange, swarmed and swam through the seas.

Then the King turned to the skies.

With a Breath and a Word he spoke. And flapping and flocking, life burst through the clouds as well!

And as for the land, surely there should be life there too.

So, with a Breath and a Word, God spoke. And paws padded, and hooves hammered, and tiny insect feet skittered and scattered along the ground.

And when God the King looked at all he had created, he saw that it was good.

Good, but not finished. For everything the King made was made ready for the crown of his creation – for his people.

And so, with a Breath and a Word, he made the first man and the first woman. Made them in his image, to be in charge of the fish and the birds and the animals.

"Fill the earth with life," he told them. "Feast on fruit and grain. This world is my gift—my blessing to you. Take care of it for me."

And, with that, the King rested. And because he was a King who loved his people and knew just what they needed, he set aside that day of rest for them to rest too.

And that was very good!

2. THE FIRST REBELLION
GENESIS 3

God the King wanted to make a home for the first man, Adam, and the first woman, Eve. So he found a plot in a spot called Eden, and there he planted a garden.

"Spring!" said the King. And up the from the ground sprouted trees, beautiful to behold and bursting with fruit.

Then, in the middle of the garden, God grew two special trees. One was the tree of life. The delicious fruit from this tree meant that Adam and Eve could live for ever. But the other tree was very different.

"You can eat the fruit from any tree, including the tree of life," God said, "except for this one – the tree of the knowledge of good and evil. For if you eat from this tree, you will die."

No one knows how long Adam and Eve lived there, eating fruit from the trees and meeting each evening with their loving King.

But one day, Eve was approached by the serpent – a crafty creature who did not respect the rule of the King and had decided to rebel against him.

Keen that others should join his rebellion, the serpent asked Eve what sounded, at first, like a completely innocent question.

"Did God really say that you must not eat the lovely fruit in this garden?"

"Oh no," she replied. "It's just the tree of the knowledge of good and evil that we must avoid. If we eat the fruit from that one, or even touch it, we will die."

"Ridiculous!" cried the serpent. "You won't die!"

That was his first lie. And the second soon followed.

"Here's the real reason," he whispered. "God alone decides what is good and what is evil. If you eat the fruit from the tree, you will also be able to decide what is good and what is evil. And the last thing God wants is for you to be God too!"

Eve stared at the fruit. It looked delicious. And if eating it would make her like God, well, all the better!

She believed the serpent's lies. And, lured into his rebellion, she ate the fruit. Then she gave it to Adam, who ate it too.

At once, their eyes were opened. They saw that they were naked. And that did not seem good. So they sewed clothes out of fig leaves. And when God came looking for them that evening, they hid from their loving King.

"Where are you?" God called.

"We're naked! And we're afraid!" Adam trembled.

God knew what they had done. "You ate from the tree, didn't you?" he said, sadly.

Adam blamed Eve. Eve blamed the serpent. And, in the end, God punished them all.

"Serpent," he said, "you will slither along the earth. Eve, you will feel pain in childbirth. And Adam, you will have to wrestle with the ground to grow your food."

Then God sent Adam and Eve away from their beautiful garden home. But not before he gave them something else – a clue to the way he would end the rebellion for ever.

"There will be a child," he promised. "The serpent will bruise his heel, yes. But in the end, that child will crush the serpent's head."

And with that promise, Adam and Eve left the garden and made their way out into the world.

3. THE ARK AND THE RAINBOW
GENESIS 6 v 1 – 9 v 17

When God the King made the world, he carved out a safe place between the waters above and the waters below, where his people could live.

But when Adam and Eve decided to choose for themselves what was good and what was evil, the rebellion that had started as a lie on the serpent's tongue and fruit in their mouths spread throughout the world, so that it was no longer a safe place for humans to enjoy.

One of their sons murdered the other, and within ten generations, violence had overwhelmed the world. Evil was all anyone could think about or do.

That made God sad – and sorry that he had put men and women on earth in the first place.

If they did not want a safe place, God decided that he would give them what they wanted. He would let the waters above crash down upon the waters below and take away that space with a great flood – and every living thing with it.

And yet... there was the loving promise God had made – of a child who would crush the serpent's head to set things right.

There was a man called Noah.

Noah didn't choose for himself what was good and what was evil. Noah did what God said was good. And he refused to do what God said was evil.

So God told Noah about the flood.

And God told Noah how to build an ark.

Then God told Noah how he wanted him to fill it. With two of every kind of animal. And with every member of his family. And with food enough to feed them all.

It was a huge job. But Noah knew that if God had told him to do it, it must be the right thing to do. And that if God promised to protect him, God would.

So, when the ark was finished and filled from stem to stern with animals and family and food, God shut the door, and the rain began to fall.

For 40 days and nights, the waters above poured down, the waters below rose up, and every living thing drowned. Apart from everyone in the ark, that is. For, just as God had promised, they stayed perfectly safe.

For 150 days, the ark floated on the waters, high above the highest mountains. Then God sent a wind to blow, and, wave by wave, the waters went down until the boat landed, at last, on dry ground. And stopped on the top of a mountain called Ararat.

Noah waited. Then, keen to see if the waters had washed below the trees, he sent out a raven – and then a dove. But neither found a branch on which to land. He sent out another dove. And when that dove returned, first, with an olive branch, and then not at all, Noah knew that the waters had finally washed away.

"Come out of the ark!" God called, at last. "Have babies and fill the world with life!"

And with that, God the King made another promise.

"I will never flood the whole of the earth again."

And in the sky, God put a rainbow to show that he really meant it!

4. THE TOO-TALL TOWER
GENESIS 11 v 1-9

Noah had been a good man.
And the flood had given the world a new start.
But that didn't stop men and women following in the
footsteps of Adam and Eve. They still wanted to choose
for themselves what was good and what was evil. And
they still wanted to be kings of their own lives instead
of letting God be their loving King.
And so, some time after the flood, a great group
of people travelled west and settled on a flat plain
in a place called Shinar.

"Let's build a magnificent city," they said. "And,
in the middle, let's raise a tall tower – one that
will reach right up into the heavens. Then
everyone will know just how amazing we are!"
They were planning to make a kingdom
without the King – a place where *they* would be
known as "great" instead of God.
And so they began to build. And because everyone
in the world spoke the very same language,
it was no problem.
"Let's make a new kind of brick, hard as stone,"
one builder suggested.
"Great idea," another builder replied.
"And let's stick the bricks together with this new-fangled
bitumen stuff," said a third builder.
And the fourth builder replied with a nod and a "Got it!"

Big and bigger the city expanded. Tall and taller the tower rose. And wide and wider grew the grins of the people who came up with the idea in the first place.

"No one is as incredible as us!" they boasted.

God listened in on their conversation. Their plan sounded impressive, but God knew that, without him, it just wouldn't work.

So God came up with what may have been the world's very first practical joke – a joke that would teach the people an important, humbling lesson.

And, with that, God confused their languages, so they could no longer understand each other.

A "Pass me the bricks!" from one builder was met with a "Huh?" and a puzzled look from another.

A "Spread that bitumen!" from a third builder was met with a shrug from the fourth.

Unable to understand each other, the people abandoned their project and wandered off, in different directions, across the earth, where God would carry on building his own kingdom.

And the place where they had hoped to make a name for themselves was called Babel – a reminder that God had confused their language and a monument to nothing more than their arrogance and their pride.

5. THE KING MAKES A NATION
GENESIS 12 v 1-9; 15 v 1-6; 17 v 1-16; 18 v 1-15; 21 v 1-7

From Babel, people wandered all across the world.

Some went to a place they called Ur. Then, one day, God spoke to a man who lived there. A man called Abram.

"Follow me!" God said to Abram, "and I will lead you to a new land that you can call your own.

"If you do, I will make a great nation from you and your children. And that nation will be a blessing to the world!"

Blessing? What kind of blessing?

For a start, the world would be able to see what it meant for God to be the loving King of a specific people in a specific place. But there was more. God had made a promise, remember? A child would come to destroy the power of evil. And that child had to come from somewhere. So God chose Abram to be the father of a people that God would call his own – a people from whom that child would one day come.

There was just one slightly awkward problem.

Abram was 75. His wife, Sarai, was 65. And they had no children. Not one!

Still, Abram trusted God.

With his family and his animals and everything he owned, he left his country and followed God to the land of Canaan. And when he arrived, he built an altar and thanked God for his new home.

Abram settled in the land. Years passed, but still he had no children. And the question remained: How could he be the father of a nation, without a child?

So God came to Abram again.

"Step outside your tent," God told him, "and look up into the sky. Can you count the stars? Of course not. There are far too many.

"One day, Abram, your children and grandchildren and all their children, down through the ages, will outnumber even the stars in the sky!"

Then God made a covenant with Abram. It was a special relationship, a set of promises, that kings often made with their people in those days. A set of promises that said, "I will do 'this' for you, and you will do 'that' for me".

In this "kingly covenant promise", God vowed to give Abram a child who would be the start of a huge nation, and a special land for that nation to live in. And all God wanted was for Abram to trust him.

So Abram did.

And when he was 99 years old and Sarai was 89, God gave them new names. Abram became Abraham, which means "father of many nations". And Sarai became Sarah, which means "princess". And he gave them a new promise too – that some of the people from their family would be kings!

Shortly after that, they had three visitors.

Abraham welcomed them and prepared a lovely meal for them – cakes and curds and cooked calf!

"Where is your wife, Sarah?" the visitors asked.

"Right there, in the tent," Abraham replied.

"We will visit you again next year," the visitors said, chasing the cake crumbs from their laps. "And by that time, Sarah will have given birth to a child."

And that was when someone laughed.

Not Abraham. And not the visitors. No, it was Sarah, who had been listening from inside the tent.

"Why did Sarah laugh?" asked the visitors. "Nothing is too hard for God."

And, sure enough, it wasn't. For within the year, Sarah did indeed have a son.

And they called the boy "laughter", for that is what his name, Isaac, means!

6. THE NATION GROWS
GENESIS 22 v 1-19; 24; 25 v 19 – 26 v 5; 27 – 33

The boy Isaac. The child called "laughter". It was a start. A small start. But it was the beginning of a nation where God would be King.

Then God asked Abraham to sacrifice his son, Isaac. And that was no laughing matter.

Still, Abraham trusted God. So up the mountain they went, father and son. With wood and fire for the altar.

"Where is the sacrifice?" Isaac asked.

And all Abraham could say was that God would provide.

And so God did. For as Abraham raised the knife above his son, he heard a voice from heaven and saw a ram trapped in some thorns. God had provided the ram to be sacrificed instead of Isaac.

"God knows your trust is in him alone," said the voice, "for you were willing to give him your only son".

And those words were not only a celebration of Abraham's faith in God's promise but also a picture of how God himself would one day sacrifice his own Son – that promised child (remember?), bruised by the serpent to crush the serpent's head.

When the time was right, Abraham sent a servant to find Isaac a wife – back to his homeland and his own people.

Outside the city of Nahor, near a well, the servant met a beautiful woman called Rebekah, who kindly offered to water his camels.

Rebekah and Isaac were married, and she gave birth to twin sons. Esau, the firstborn, was covered with red hair. And smooth-skinned Jacob was born second, hanging onto his brother's heel.

The boys grew, and as they did, God repeated the kingly covenant promise to Isaac that he had made to his father, Abraham.

"Live in this land, and your children will outnumber the stars in the sky and be a blessing to the world."

The problem was that the two boys hardly seemed to be a blessing even to their family! And it did not help that Isaac preferred Esau, a great hunter, and that Rebekah preferred Jacob, who stayed in the tent by her side.

That hanging-onto-the-heel rivalry between the twins had already erupted on a day when Esau came into the tent, famished, and Jacob was brewing up a lovely stew.

"Gimme some of that!" Esau demanded.

"I'll swap you for it," Jacob replied. "You're the oldest, so how about you give me the right to run the family when Father dies?"

"Fine!" Esau grunted. "Because *I'll* die if I don't get something to eat!"

That "right" had to come with Isaac's blessing, though. And things between the brothers got much worse when Rebekah helped Jacob to fool his father and steal that blessing for himself.

Esau was furious and vowed to kill his brother.

So Jacob ran for his life. And when he could run no further, he fell to the ground, grabbed a stone for his pillow and dreamed.

He saw a ladder reaching up to heaven, filled with angels. And God himself above it all. And that is when God made the same kingly covenant promise to Jacob that he had made to Abraham and Isaac.

"This land is yours. You will return to it. Your children – more than you can count – will bless the earth. And I will watch over you."

And so God did.

Jacob left that place and went back to Abraham's homeland and his mother's brother, Laban.

His uncle Laban tricked him into marrying not one of his daughters but two.

And, yes, there were dangers and adventures along the way.

But God brought Jacob through them all, helped him to make peace with Esau, and led Jacob back, at last, to the land of promise.

7. THE NATION MOVES!
GENESIS 37; 39 – 47

When God the King made his kingly covenant promise with Abraham, Isaac and Jacob, he promised to take care of the nation that would come from them. And he did that in some surprising ways!

Jacob had twelve sons, but Joseph was the child of his favourite wife, Rachael. Jacob made Joseph a beautiful many-coloured coat, and that made his brothers jealous. Well, that and Joseph's dreams.

In one dream, his brother's sheaves of wheat bowed down to Joseph's sheaf. In another dream, they were stars, bowing before him.

The dreams came from God, but all that Joseph's brothers could see was a puffed-up boy who needed to be taught a lesson.

So one day, when they were all in the fields together, they grabbed Joseph, tore off his coat and dumped him in a pit. They wanted to kill him, but when a caravan of Ishmaelite traders came camel-ing by, they sold him, instead, for 20 silver coins. Then they dipped his coat in blood and took it to their father, claiming that an animal had eaten him.

Jacob was devastated. But God had promised to watch out for Jacob's children, hadn't he? And so God did, as step by step, he made Joseph's dreams come true.

The Ishmaelites carried Joseph to Egypt and sold him as a slave to Potiphar, captain of the guard in Pharaoh's palace. God blessed everything Joseph did, and Potiphar put Joseph in charge of his household.

Sadly, however, Potiphar's wife told lies about Joseph, and Potiphar had him thrown in prison.

Things looked bad. But there was God's kingly covenant promise, remember?

Pharaoh's cupbearer and baker also found themselves in prison. And when they each had a puzzling dream, God told Joseph exactly what those dreams meant – and they came true!

So, when Pharaoh himself had a puzzling dream, the cupbearer remembered Joseph, and Joseph was brought before the king of all Egypt.

Joseph, of course, was under the protection of an even greater King. So, when Pharaoh told Joseph his dream about seven skinny cows eating seven fat cows and seven skinny ears of corn eating seven fat ears, God the King told Joseph exactly what that dream meant: seven years of good crops followed by seven years of famine.

Pharaoh was so impressed with Joseph's answer that he put him in charge of storing up the crops in the seven good years so there would be plenty to eat later. And God blessed that work too.

After seven years, the famine struck, reaching even to the land of Canaan, where Joseph's family lived. And it wasn't long before his brothers were sent to buy food in Egypt and found themselves face to face with the brother they had sold into slavery.

Because of the passing years and his fine Egyptian clothes, they did not recognise Joseph. But he recognised them. So he tested them. And when he was sure that they had changed, he showed them who he really was.

They were terrified, but Joseph made it clear that God had used all that had happened to save the family. So down to Egypt came God's people, with plenty to eat and room to grow into the nation God had planned.

And God the loving King kept his promise to watch over his people.

8. A BULRUSH BASKET AND A BURNING BUSH

EXODUS 1 v 1 – 4 v 16

Seventy. That's how many members of Joseph's family were saved from the famine and went to live in Egypt. For God the King had made a kingly covenant promise to Abraham, Isaac and Jacob to watch over the nation he had created.

It still wasn't much of a "nation", though, was it? Just 70 people.

But time passed. And year after year, and child by child, those 70 people grew into the huge nation that God had promised. And it looked as if there just might be more children of Abraham than stars in the sky or dust on the earth.

That's how it seemed to a new pharaoh, anyway: one who had forgotten about what Joseph had done and could only worry that the descendants of Joseph's family – the Hebrews, as they were called – might threaten his kingdom.

So he made them his slaves, building his great cities. But the harder he treated them, the more their numbers grew. Finally, he gave the awful command that every newborn Hebrew boy should be drowned in the River Nile.

Pharaoh thought he was the most powerful king of all. What he did not know was that an even more powerful King was watching over the Hebrew people. And one of those people was a very clever woman with a little baby boy.

She built him a basket boat out of bulrushes, tarred it all over to keep out the water, set it afloat among the Nile river reeds, and sent her daughter to watch over it.

When Pharaoh's daughter discovered the basket, and the baby inside it, all seemed lost. But she felt sorry for the child and decided to keep him. Thinking quickly, the baby's sister called out, "I know a woman who could feed him for you!"

And so the child's own mother cared for him until he was old enough to be adopted by the princess – who named him Moses.

Moses grew up in Pharaoh's palace, but he was always a Hebrew at heart. One day, when he saw an Egyptian beating a Hebrew, Moses killed the Egyptian. Fearful that news of his deed would reach Pharaoh's ears, Moses fled to the land of Midian and lived there, as a shepherd, for 40 years.

And that is when he stumbled across a bush. A special bush. A bush that burned but did not burn up. And from that bush came these words…

"I am the God of Abraham, Isaac and Jacob. I have heard the sad cries of my suffering people. I have come to help them. And you, Moses, must go to Pharaoh and tell him to set my people free."

Moses had plenty of excuses: "I'm a nobody! What if they ask who sent me? Why should they believe me? I'm no good at speaking!"

And God had plenty of answers: "You're my servant. Tell them that 'I Am' sent you. They'll believe you when they see the miracles you do. And your brother Aaron is a great speaker, so he can help you!

"Now, no more excuses!" said God. "Go! Go and tell Pharaoh to set my people free!"

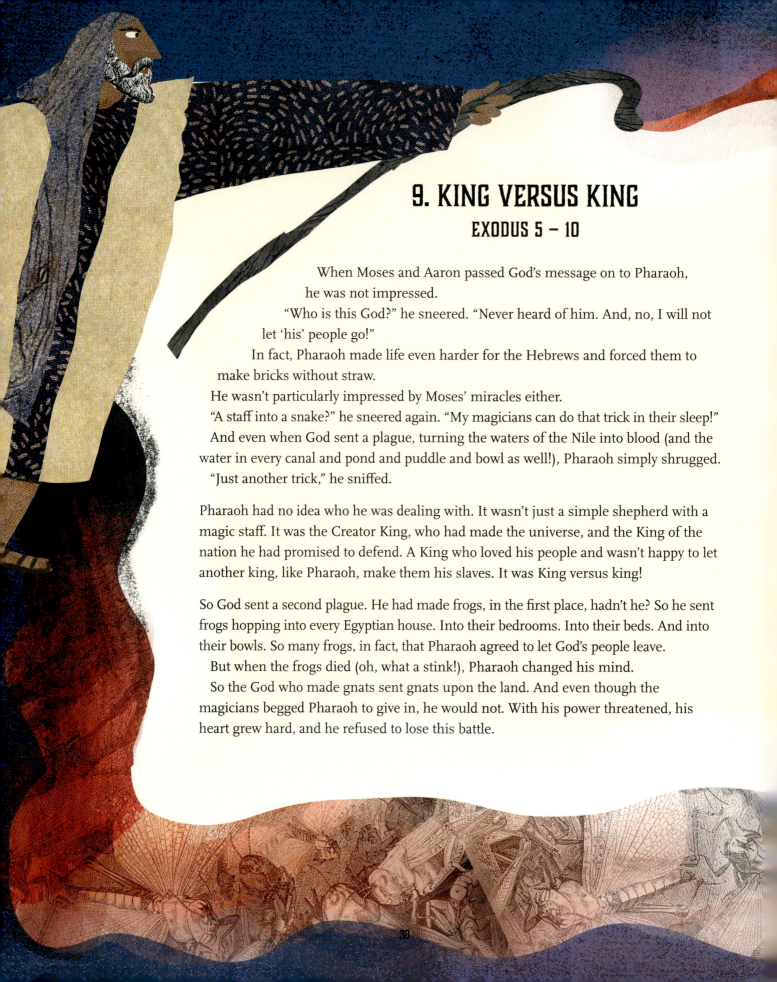

9. KING VERSUS KING
EXODUS 5 – 10

When Moses and Aaron passed God's message on to Pharaoh, he was not impressed.

"Who is this God?" he sneered. "Never heard of him. And, no, I will not let 'his' people go!"

In fact, Pharaoh made life even harder for the Hebrews and forced them to make bricks without straw.

He wasn't particularly impressed by Moses' miracles either.

"A staff into a snake?" he sneered again. "My magicians can do that trick in their sleep!"

And even when God sent a plague, turning the waters of the Nile into blood (and the water in every canal and pond and puddle and bowl as well!), Pharaoh simply shrugged.

"Just another trick," he sniffed.

Pharaoh had no idea who he was dealing with. It wasn't just a simple shepherd with a magic staff. It was the Creator King, who had made the universe, and the King of the nation he had promised to defend. A King who loved his people and wasn't happy to let another king, like Pharaoh, make them his slaves. It was King versus king!

So God sent a second plague. He had made frogs, in the first place, hadn't he? So he sent frogs hopping into every Egyptian house. Into their bedrooms. Into their beds. And into their bowls. So many frogs, in fact, that Pharaoh agreed to let God's people leave.

But when the frogs died (oh, what a stink!), Pharaoh changed his mind.

So the God who made gnats sent gnats upon the land. And even though the magicians begged Pharaoh to give in, he would not. With his power threatened, his heart grew hard, and he refused to lose this battle.

So the God who made flies sent flies upon the land. And swarms of them flew into the houses of the Egyptians. But the Hebrew houses were spared.

"All right, go!" Pharaoh agreed. "Just take away these flies!"

But when the flies had gone, again he changed his mind.

So the God who made horses and camels and cows made the animals of Egypt die. But the Hebrew animals were spared. And Pharaoh's heart grew harder still.

So the God who made dust told Moses to throw dust in the air. And when it landed on the Egyptians, it made painful sores appear on their bodies. The magicians were all in pain, and they begged Pharaoh to admit defeat. But he would not.

So the God who made rain and snow sent lightning and thunder and hail upon the land, crushing the crops of the Egyptians. But sparing the Hebrews' barley and flax.

"Make it stop!" pleaded Pharaoh. "And your people can go."

But as soon as the sun shone, he changed his mind again.

The hail had crushed the barley and flax, but the wheat had only just begun to sprout. So the God who made locusts sent locusts to devour the wheat and the trees and every other green growing thing that remained.

"Go!" Pharaoh cried.

But when God sent a wind to blow the locusts into the sea, again Pharaoh changed his mind.

So the God who made light removed the light from the land and plunged Egypt into darkness.

"Leave!" Pharaoh cried, only to change his mind once more.

So God the King, the God who gave the breath of life, told Moses what he would do next...

10. THE REDEEMER KING
EXODUS 11 – 12

Pharaoh the king would not budge. He was determined to keep hold of his slaves, even in the face of the plagues that God the King had sent.

But God wasn't just the King of the nation he loved. He was also the Creator King.

So, in order to rescue his people, the God who had given the breath of life in the first place decided to take that life away.

"At midnight," he told Moses, "I will visit the Egyptians, and every one of their firstborn children, from the palace down to the humblest dwelling, will die. And every firstborn animal too. But I will spare my own people. This is what they must do.

"Every household must choose a lamb – a perfect lamb.

"At twilight, everyone must kill their lamb.

"Then they must take a bunch of hyssop, dip it in the blood of the lamb and spread the blood on the doorposts and the lintels of their houses.

"Next, they must eat the lamb. No bones broken. Roasted. Not boiled or raw.

"Bread without yeast and bitter herbs must also be a part of the meal.

"And they must eat it in a hurry, with their belts fastened, their sandals on and their staffs in their hands.

"Then, at midnight, when I visit the land, I will *pass over* the houses with the blood of the lamb on their doors and lintels, and the firstborn in those houses will not die."

God told Moses that his people should eat that Passover meal every year so they would never forget what he had done for them. And so they would always remember that he was not only the Creator King and the King of their nation but also their Redeemer King.

What is a redeemer?
It's someone who
sets someone else free,
usually at a great cost. The
lives of all those little lambs,
whose blood was painted on
the doorways, was the price that
set the Hebrews free. But it was
also a picture of the price that God
himself would one day pay when the
blood of his own firstborn Son – the
Lamb of God – would be shed to crush
the serpent's head and set everyone free
from sin and death.

God's people followed his instructions, and,
sure enough, at midnight, every Egyptian
firstborn died. But God passed over the houses
with a lamb's blood on the doors and lintels, so every
Hebrew home was spared.

Pharaoh's own son was among the dead.
And so, with his will broken along with his heart,
Pharaoh let God's people leave.

11. THE TRIUMPH OF THE KING
EXODUS 13 v 17 – 15 v 3

And so the Hebrews escaped at last from Egypt, with their triumphant God and King leading his people – in a pillar of cloud by day and a pillar of fire by night to light the way.

By the time they reached the Red Sea, however, Pharaoh had once again changed his mind.

"What have I done?" he cried. "I have lost my slaves!"

And so, with 600 chariots, he chased the Hebrews to the edge of the sea.

But God the King would not have his victory taken from him. The pillar of cloud moved from the front of the people to the back, blocking Pharaoh's view.

"Raise your staff!" God commanded Moses. "Stretch your hand over the sea. And watch it part!"

And when Moses did, God sent a strong east wind to blow across the water. Sure enough, the sea split, with a dry path down the middle so that God's people could escape to the other side.

Through the parted sea they rushed, with the water making a wall to their right and to their left. The Egyptian chariots followed. But God appeared above the Egyptians – in fire and in cloud – and threw their army into a great panic.

"Retreat!" they cried. "Their God fights for them!"

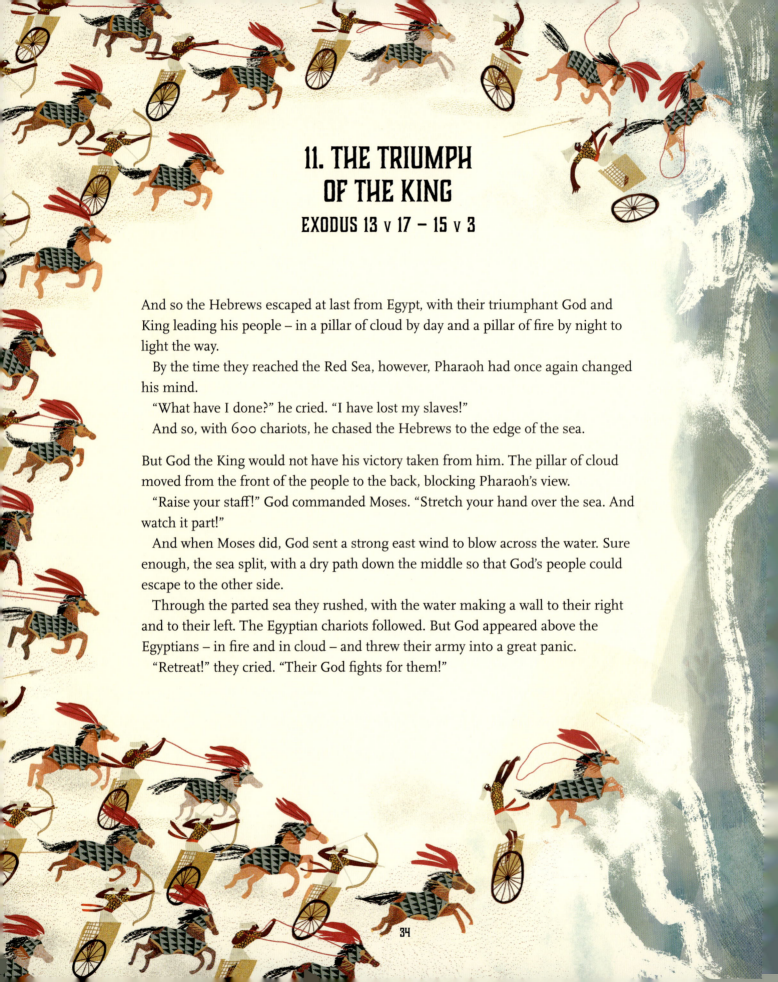

But it was too late. Their chariot wheels were clogged with mud and would not turn.

And so, just as the last of his people had safely crossed, God told Moses to stretch his hand over the sea again. The watery walls crashed down on the Egyptians. Every chariot was crushed. Not one soldier survived. And the victory of God the King over the earthly king who dared to challenge him was complete.

God's people danced. God's people sang.

"Our God has triumphed. We will sing his praise, for Pharaoh's chariots and his army have been thrown into the sea!"

God, their Redeemer King, had set them free!

12. ANOTHER KINGLY COVENANT
EXODUS 15 v 22 – 17 v 7; 19 – 24

God the King had defeated Pharaoh, the king of Egypt, and now God's people were free! So off they headed, back to the land he had promised to Abraham, Isaac and Jacob.

When they were hungry, God fed them – with miraculous bread, called manna, in the morning and fresh, fat quail at night.

And when they were thirsty, God told Moses to throw a log into water that was nasty and undrinkable – and the water became very tasty indeed! Then, later, God told Moses to strike a rock at Horeb, and more water streamed out for them to drink!

And when they came to Mount Sinai, the very same mountain where Moses had seen the burning bush, God gave them something else – a new kingly covenant.

It's what kings did in those days, remember?

"I will do 'this' for you, and you will do 'that' for me."

God's people camped around the base of the mountain. And up the mountain Moses went.

"This is what I want you to tell my people," God said.

"You saw what I did to the Egyptians – how, like a great eagle, I picked you up and carried you out of slavery. Everything on earth is mine, but you will be my treasure, my special people, if you will listen to my voice and obey the laws I give you. You will be my kingdom of priests, my holy nation – set apart to bring the rest of the world to me!"

Moses told the people, and the people agreed. All that was left now was for Moses to climb back up the mountain and to receive God's laws for his people – loving laws from a good and loving King – so that they could live in the best possible way.

Around the mountain the people gathered. And out of the cloud that covered the mountain came thunder and lightning and the blast of a great trumpet. Terrified, the people trembled. And then, in fire, God came down upon the mountain.

The mountain shook. Smoke rose from it, like from an enormous furnace. Thunder and trumpets blasted louder and louder still.

Then, bravely, Moses climbed up the mountain to receive God's laws.

There were ten laws to start with...

1. GOD'S PEOPLE MUST WORSHIP GOD AND HIM ONLY

2. THEY MUST NOT MAKE ANY IDOLS TO WORSHIP

3. THEY MUST NOT TREAT GOD'S NAME AS IF IT MEANS NOTHING

4. THEY MUST KEEP ONE DAY FOR REST, JUST AS GOD RESTED AFTER HE HAD MADE THE WORLD

5. THEY MUST RESPECT THEIR PARENTS

6. THEY MUST NOT MURDER ANYONE

7. THEY MUST BE FAITHFUL TO THE PERSON THEY MARRY

8. THEY MUST NOT STEAL

9. THEY MUST NOT LIE

10. THEY MUST NOT BE JEALOUS OF WHAT THEIR NEIGHBOURS OWN

But there were more laws, as well. Many more. Laws about worship. Laws about paying for things that had been wrecked or ruined. Laws about treating people fairly. Laws about special holy days.

Then God told Moses that if his people would obey these laws, he would help them move back into the land that he had given to Abraham, Isaac and Jacob.

It took a long time, but when Moses came back down the mountain, he gathered the people together and read them the Book of the Covenant – the laws of God their King. And, as one, the people said, "We have heard. And we promise to obey."

13. REBELLION IN THE WILDERNESS
EXODUS 24 v 12 – 32 v 35; NUMBERS 14 v 1-38

God had set his people free and made a new kingly covenant promise with them. Sadly, it didn't take long for them to break their side of the promise.

Moses went back up the mountain to speak with God. God gave Moses instructions on how to build a special tent called a tabernacle – where God would live with his people and where they could worship him.

Moses was up on that mountain for 40 days and nights. And the people began to wonder if he was ever going to come back down again. So, instead of trusting the God who had set them free and the man he had used to do that, they broke the covenant promise they had just made to God, and they made an idol to worship as their god instead!

They collected as much jewellery as they could. They melted it down and made a golden statue of a calf. Then they worshipped the statue, saying, "*This* is the god who brought us out of Egypt".

And who did they choose to lead them in all of this? Aaron! Moses' own brother, who had spoken to Pharaoh for him.

God knew this was happening, of course. He was heartbroken. And furious. He told Moses what was going on. And then he told Moses what he was going to do about it.

"I will destroy these people," God said, "and make a new nation for myself from you and your children!"

It sounded a lot like a kingly covenant promise that God had already made. And Moses reminded God of that.

"That was your promise to Abraham, Isaac and Jacob," he said. "To bless the world through their descendants. By your great power, you saved them from the Egyptians. Please don't destroy them now."

So God held back his anger and did not destroy his people. But when Moses went down the mountain and saw what the people had done, he struggled to control his anger too. He smashed the two tablets God had given him – the tablets upon which God himself had written his law.

Many people were punished that day, but, sadly, that was not the end of what turned out to be their constant complaining and grumbling as they made their way to the land God had promised them.

"There's not enough to eat!"

"There's not enough to drink!"

"When are we going to get there?" (Well, nobody said that, but they might as well have!)

And even as they were about to enter the land, there was moaning and more moaning.

Moses sent twelve spies into the land, to see what it was like. Ten of them came back with tales of walled cities and giants too big to beat. But two of them, Joshua and Caleb, argued that, with God's help, they could indeed claim the land for themselves.

Sadly, the people ignored Joshua and Caleb's advice and wished they had stayed in Egypt.

So God sent them to wander in the wilderness for 40 years, until only Joshua and Caleb and a new (and hopefully more trusting) generation survived.

Finally, it was time to enter the land of promise!

14. THE KING WHO TAKES CARE OF HIS PEOPLE

JOSHUA 1 – 6

When Moses died, God made Joshua the leader of his people. That's right, Joshua, who had been sent as a spy into the land of promise. Joshua, who, along with Caleb, believed that God would help his people to take the land.

And that is exactly what God told him.

"Every place where you place your foot, I will give you!" said God. "Obey the laws I gave to Moses. Study them, day and night. Do what they say. Then be strong and brave, for I will be with you."

God's people had yet to cross the Jordan River into the land of promise, for on the other side there stood the great walled city of Jericho. And Joshua needed to know more about it.

So he sent two of his own spies to check it out. When they had sneaked into the city, they stayed in the house of a woman called Rahab – a house with a window built into the city walls. When the king of Jericho discovered that they were there, he sent his soldiers to seize them. But clever Rahab hid the spies on her roof and covered them with stalks of flax; then she told the soldiers that they had escaped into the countryside.

Off the soldiers ran, while Rahab had a secret word with the spies.

"We have heard what happened in Egypt," she said. "And we know that your God will help you defeat our people too. So promise me that you will remember me and spare my family when you do."

The spies agreed and told her to tie a red cord in the window during the attack.

"When our soldiers see this," they promised, "no one in your house will be harmed".

Then Rahab threw a rope out of her window. Down the spies climbed. And back to Joshua they went.

Three surprises followed, as God led his people into the land of promise.

First, much as he had done when he parted the Red Sea, God made the waters of the Jordan River split in two. And, again, his people walked across on dry ground.

When it came to conquering the city of Jericho, God had another surprise in store for them.

"March once round the city for six days," God said. "Soldiers silent and priests blowing trumpets. And on the seventh day, march round seven times. Then, when the trumpets have blasted, everybody must SHOUT as loud as they can!"

So they did – and when they shouted on that seventh day, the walls came tumbling down!

The soldiers conquered the city. And, just as promised, Rahab and her family were kept safe.

And that's where the third surprise comes in. Remember the special child God promised to Adam and Eve – the one who would crush the serpent's head? Well, if you look closely at the list of people who were ancestors of that child, you will find a name you recognise. Not Joshua. And not Caleb either.

No, the name you will find is the name of someone who lived in Jericho. Who had a house with a window in the wall. The name you will find – surprise! – is Rahab.

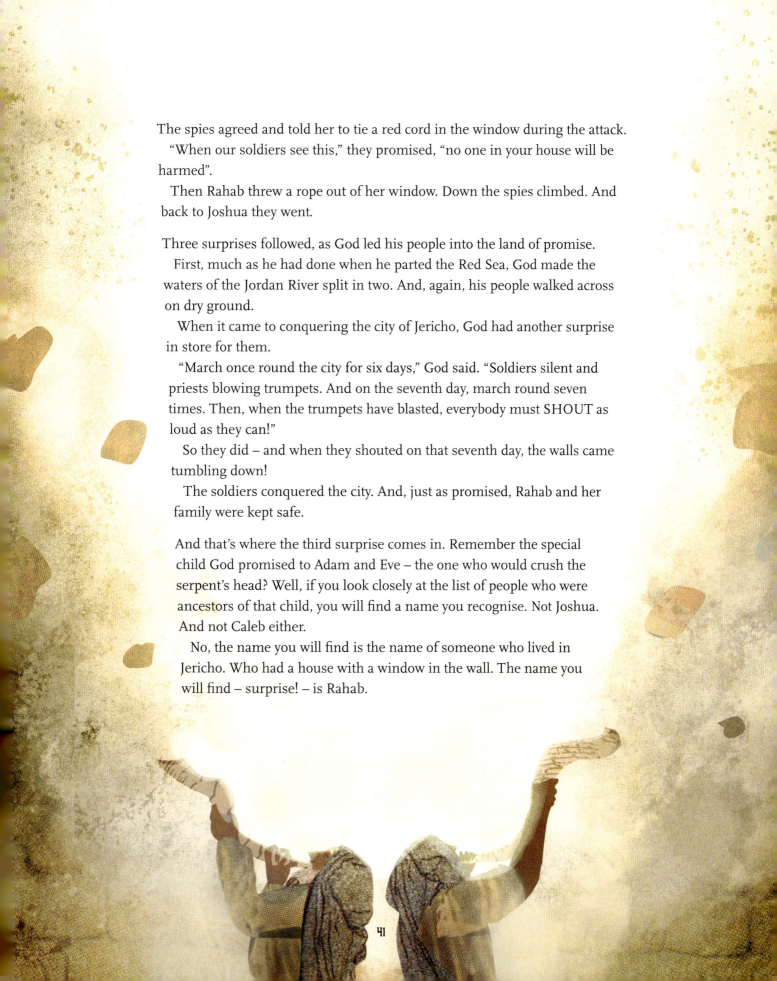

15. THE KING AND HIS JUDGES
JUDGES 2 – 4; 6 – 7; 13 – 16; 1 SAMUEL 3 – 7

City by city, kingdom by kingdom, God's people took hold of the land he had promised them. Then they divided it up between the twelve tribes descended from the sons of Jacob.

But because they were disobedient to God their King, they were unable to conquer the whole of the land. And those undefeated "neighbours" – who were actually more like enemies – proved to be nothing but trouble for them for many years to come.

When God's people obeyed him, things were fine. But when they disobeyed him – usually by worshipping the false gods of their enemies – those enemies would defeat them in battle and make their life a misery.

So they would turn back to God and beg for his help, and God would choose someone to save them from their enemies – someone called a judge. Then, when the enemies were defeated, things would be fine until the judge died and the people disobeyed God again. Here are the most famous judges…

JUDGE: EHUD – ENEMY: MOABITES
Ehud was a left-handed man. He tricked the guards of the Moabite king, Eglon, by hiding a left-handed sword on his right thigh under his cloak where they wouldn't expect to see one. And, using that sword, he killed King Eglon and lost his sword in the fat king's belly!

JUDGE: DEBORAH – ENEMY: CANAANITES
That's right, women could be judges too. And, in Deborah's case, a prophet, as well! Under her leadership, God's people defeated Jabin, the king of Canaan. And his commander, Sisera, was killed by yet another woman, Jael, who hammered a tent peg through his head.

JUDGE: GIDEON – ENEMY: MIDIANITES

When God's people disobeyed him again, the Midianites overcame them and took all the food they grew. So God chose Gideon as a judge. And with only 300 men – and torches and trumpets and jars – he defeated the Midianite army!

JUDGE: SAMSON – ENEMY: PHILISTINES

Samson was a Nazirite, which meant he promised God that he would not drink alcohol, touch anything dead or cut his hair. God gifted him with great strength, which he used to fight the Philistines. He tied torches to the tails of 300 foxes to set their fields alight. He killed 1,000 Philistines with the jawbone of a donkey. But he was undone when he revealed to a woman called Delilah that his strength would disappear if his hair was cut. She told the Philistines, and Samson was captured and led away in chains. They blinded him and put him in prison. But as his hair grew back, so did his strength. And when they dragged him into their arena to mock him, he pushed over two pillars holding up the building, and he and the Philistines died together as it came crashing down.

JUDGE: SAMUEL – ENEMY: PHILISTINES

Like Deborah, Samuel was a prophet as well as a judge. God spoke to him when he was just a child, serving in the tabernacle. And it was during his time that the people decided that they no longer wanted judges to rule over them. And not God either. What they wanted, instead, was a human king.

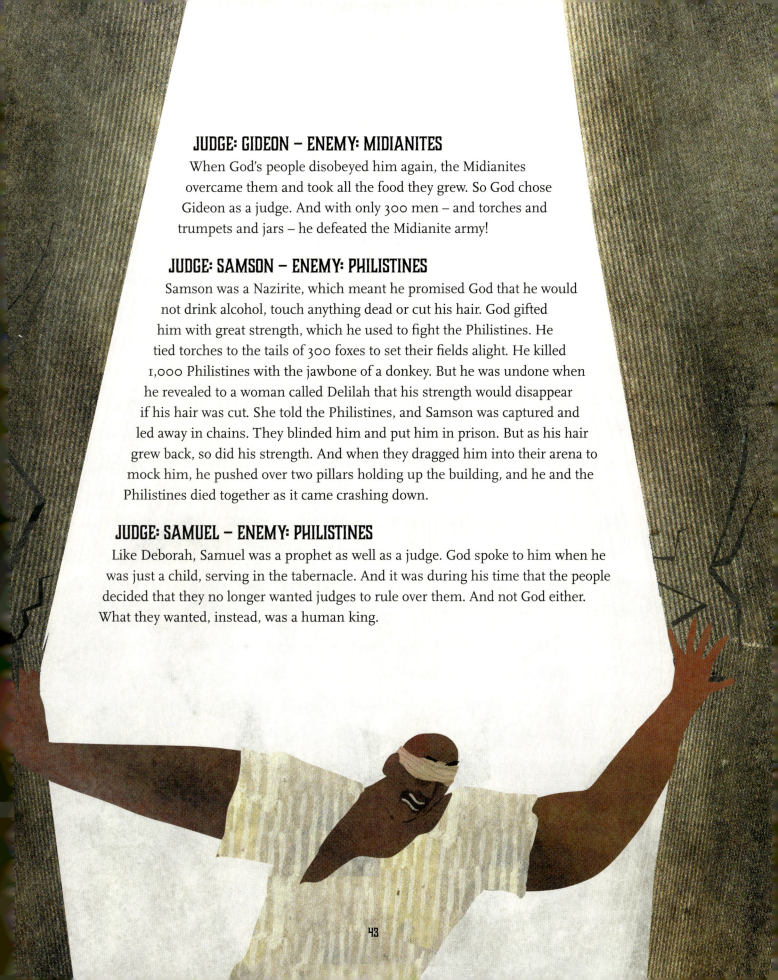

16. WE WANT A KING!
1 SAMUEL 8

"We want a king!" whined the elders of Israel.
"Everybody else has a king. Why can't we have one too?"

Samuel knew why. He was a judge – appointed by God, like Deborah and Gideon before him, to watch over Israel. And he was a prophet, who heard God's voice and passed God's messages on to his people.

So Samuel knew that the people of Israel weren't "like everybody else". God was their King. Always had been. And judges and prophets were the servants God used to care for his people.

"We want a king!" the elders whined again. "You're too old, Samuel. And the sons you have chosen to replace you are more concerned with bribes than justice. So we want a king to be our judge and lead us into battle. A king like every other nation!"

Samuel sighed. He knew that his sons were not following the path he had taught them. But when he went to God, feeling sad and rejected, God had a different view.

God had seen this before. In the garden. Before the flood. Time and time again. And that is why God said...

"It's not you they are rejecting, Samuel. It's me. I brought them out of Egypt. I set them free and parted a sea to help their escape. But even then, they made statues and worshipped other gods. So don't take this personally. It's me they no longer want to be their King."

And that is why, as he had done so many times before, God let his people make their choice.

"They can have their king," God said, "but make sure they understand exactly what that will mean".

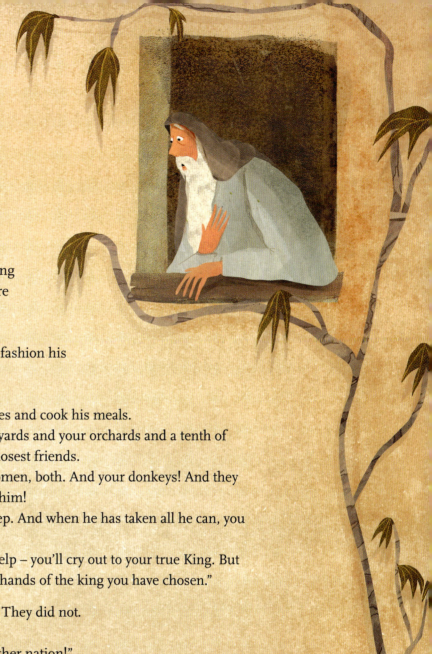

So Samuel told the elders. "You can get yourselves a king. But trust me, getting a king will be less about what you will get and more about what he will take!

"First, he will take your sons.

"They'll drive his chariots, fight his wars, fashion his weapons and plough his fields.

"He'll take your daughters next.

"They'll make his perfumes, bake his cakes and cook his meals.

"Then he'll take your fields and your vineyards and your orchards and a tenth of what you grow. And he'll give them to his closest friends.

"He'll take your servants too. Men and women, both. And your donkeys! And they won't work for you. Oh no, they'll work for him!

"And finally, he'll take a tenth of your sheep. And when he has taken all he can, you will be his slaves.

"Then, trust me, you will cry to God for help – you'll cry out to your true King. But he will not answer. He will leave you in the hands of the king you have chosen."

Did the elders listen to Samuel's warnings? They did not.

They stamped. They shouted.

"Give us a king! So we can be like every other nation!"

So Samuel told God what they had said. And God sent Samuel to find them a king.

17. THE PEOPLE'S KING
1 SAMUEL 9 – 11; 13 v 1 – 14 v 23; 15

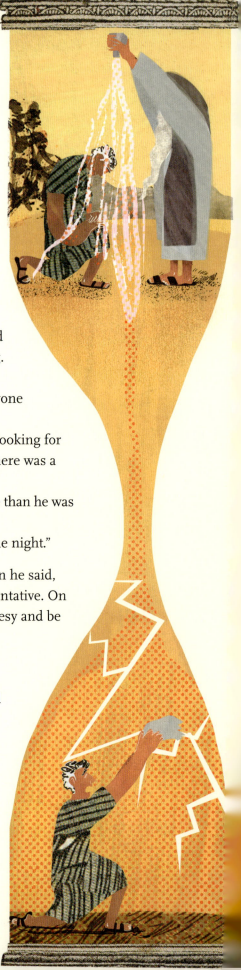

God's people wanted a king, just like the nations around them. So God gave them the kind of king they wanted: a king who *looked* like a king. A king called Saul.

Saul was tall. He stood head and shoulders above everyone. So everyone had to look up to him. The perfect position for a king!

His story started with a herd of lost donkeys. He'd spent three days looking for them. And just as he was about to give up, his servant told him that there was a prophet nearby who might be able to help.

That prophet was Samuel. And when Saul found him, he found more than he was looking for.

"Your donkeys have been found," said Samuel. "Eat with me. Stay the night."

The next day, Samuel took Saul aside. He poured oil on his head. Then he said, "God has chosen you to be king. To rule over his people as his representative. On your way back home, God's Spirit will come upon you. You will prophesy and be like a completely different man."

That's exactly what happened, but Saul did not say a word to anyone about it until Samuel called all the people to Mizpah.

"God brought you out of Egypt," Samuel said, "but you have rejected him as your King. So now he says you may choose your own king."

Saul was chosen as king, just as Samuel had said. And all went well, at first. Saul led his people in battle against the Ammonites and beat them. But when he faced the Philistines, things began to go wrong.

Saul gathered his army at a place called Gilgal. Samuel was supposed to offer a sacrifice to God before the battle. But, as Saul waited for Samuel, the Philistines gathered their army. And it was much, much bigger than he expected!

Frightened, some of Saul's soldiers sneaked away and hid. Afraid that the whole of the army would desert him, Saul decided that he could not wait for Samuel, and he made the sacrifice himself. And when Samuel arrived, he was furious.

"You fool! You have disobeyed God's command!" cried Samuel. "Your kingdom would have lasted for ever. But now God will take that kingdom from you and give it to someone whose heart desires what God's heart desires."

In spite of that, Saul defeated the Philistines and many more enemies besides. But God's decision had been made. And it was only made stronger when Saul disobeyed him again.

Saul was meant to defeat the Amalekites and destroy everything that belonged to them. But he didn't. He allowed their king to live, and he kept the best of their sheep and cattle.

When Samuel asked him what he'd done, Saul lied and said they all had been destroyed.

"So why do I hear the lowing of oxen and the bleating of sheep?" Samuel asked. And, with that, he told Saul, once again, that God had rejected him as king.

"It was the people's fault!" Saul explained (much as Adam had blamed Eve, remember?). "Please, reconsider."

But God had decided.

And the man whose heart desired what God's heart desired was already working in his father's fields, with bleating sheep of his own...

18. A KING AFTER GOD'S OWN HEART
1 SAMUEL 16 v 1-13

Saul may have looked like a king, but he didn't turn out to be the kind of king God wanted to represent him and to lead his people. So God rejected Saul and took his Spirit away from him, and that made Samuel sad.

"Don't feel bad," God told him. "I have already chosen someone else. A king after my own heart. So fill up your oil-holding horn. I'm sending you to Bethlehem, to meet a man called Jesse."

"But if Saul finds out," trembled Samuel, "he'll kill me".

"Take a bull with you," God said. "Explain that you're there to make a sacrifice. Invite Jesse. And I'll tell you whom to anoint as king."

So that's what Samuel did. He went to Bethlehem. He invited Jesse and his sons to the sacrifice. And when he took a look at tall Eliab, Jesse's oldest son, Samuel thought he'd found his man.

But God had a different plan.

"Don't focus on his height," God said to Samuel. "Or how handsome he is. For I have already rejected him. People look at what somebody is like on the outside. But I am different. I look at what's on the inside of a person. I look at their heart."

So Jesse paraded each of his sons before Samuel: Aminadab and Shammah and the rest. And as each one passed by, God told Samuel, "No".

And when the last one had been rejected, Samuel sighed and said to Jesse, "You don't happen to have any other sons, do you?"

"Well, there is my youngest," Jesse replied. "He's out in the fields, watching the sheep."

"Send for him!" said Samuel.

And when he arrived, God spoke to Samuel, plain and clear.

"This is the one!"

He was hardly more than a boy, his skin tanned from working outside. Handsome on the outside. But handsome on the inside too!

So Samuel poured oil from his horn on the head of Jesse's youngest son. At once, God's Spirit came upon him.

And God's people had a new king.

A king called David.

19. A VICTORY FOR GOD'S KING
1 SAMUEL 16 v 14 – 17 v 54

When God's Spirit left King Saul, a sad and troubling spirit came over him instead. His servants were worried about him, so they looked for someone who could play soothing music for the king.

"I know just the man!" said one of the servants. "He lives in Bethlehem. He's the son of Jesse. He's brave and well-spoken and plays the lyre beautifully. His name is David."

So the servants asked the very man God had already chosen to replace the king to come and serve him!

David's playing was so soothing that Saul made David his armour-bearer too. A very important job!

David didn't live with the king though. He went back and forth between the palace and his father's house.

One day, Jesse sent David with supplies for his older brothers, who served in the king's army.

Saul's army was camped on a hill overlooking the valley of Elah. And the Philistine army was camped in the hills on the other side.

During David's visit, someone marched out of the Philistine camp into the middle of the valley and shouted out a challenge. Someone who was a giant!

Nearly three metres* tall, he wore a bronze helmet on his head and bronze armour on his legs, and he sported a chain-mail coat. His spear was as long as a weaver's beam.

*10 feet

And his name was Goliath.

"Send someone to fight me!" he roared. "If he wins, we serve you! If I win, you serve us. Simple as that!"

The soldiers around David trembled. Not David though.

"Who does this giant think he is," David grunted, "to challenge the army of the living God? I'll fight him!"

So David was taken to King Saul.

"But you're so young," said Saul. "And this giant has been a warrior all his life."

"I've fought my battles too," said David. "When a lion or a bear took my lamb, I grabbed it by the throat and killed it. God helped me beat those beasts, and he will help me beat this Philistine too!"

"Use my armour then," said the king to his armour-bearer.

David put on the armour and shook his head. "I've never used this before," he sighed. So he took it off, and, with a staff in one hand and a sling in the other, he chose five smooth stones from a brook and set off to face the giant.

"Do you think I am a dog," Goliath roared, "that you send me this little stick-man? Come close, boy, and I will feed your flesh to the birds!"

"That is what I will do to you!" replied David. "For this battle will not be won by sword or spear but by the power of the living God, who watches over his people!"

Then David sprinted towards the giant. He slipped a stone into his sling, swung it hard and let it fly. The stone sank into Goliath's forehead, and he fell to the ground. Then, taking the giant's own sword, David killed him and cut off his head. And with a cheer, Saul's army chased after the Philistines and defeated them. And there was no doubt that God had indeed given his people the victory!

20. A KINGLY COVENANT WITH DAVID
1 SAMUEL 18 v 6-16; 2 SAMUEL 7

The giant was dead. The Philistines were defeated. And when David and King Saul returned from the battle, they were treated like heroes.

Women came out to welcome them home, singing and dancing and playing tambourines. But the song they sang surprised Saul. And not in a good way.

"Saul has killed thousands," the song went, "but David has killed tens of thousands!"

When he heard this, Saul was filled with jealousy.

"He'll want my crown next," he grumbled, unaware that God had already made that decision. And from that moment on, Saul kept an angry and watchful eye on David.

The next day, in fact, while David was playing the lyre for Saul, the king grabbed hold of a spear and hurled it at David! David ducked away from the spear, unharmed. And that is when Saul sent him away from the palace, out of his sight, to command a thousand men.

With God's help, David won battle after battle. But with each victory, King Saul grew more and more jealous. And in the end, he set out to kill David and finish the rivalry. This went on for years, and even when Saul himself died after another battle with the Philistines, his family and warriors continued to fight against David.

In the end, though, David was victorious and became king of God's people. And that is when he spoke to the prophet Nathan.

"I live in a beautiful house," David said, "but God still dwells among his people in a tent".

He meant, of course, the tabernacle that Moses had constructed, way back when God's people were still wandering through the wilderness.

"I want to build God a proper house, a temple, in which he can dwell."

This seemed like a good idea to Nathan, and he told the king so. But in the night, Nathan had a visit from God and received an entirely different answer to David's request.

"I have lived in a tent since I brought my people out of Egypt," God said. "I have travelled with them here and there. And when I appointed judges over my people, did I ask them to build me a house? No.

"As for David, I have watched over him since he was a shepherd. I have protected him from his enemies. And I have made him my king.

"Do I want David to build me a house? I do not. No, I have something better in mind. I want to make a house out of David! That's right – a house from his family that will stand for ever.

"I will love his family and discipline them when they go wrong. One of his sons will build me a temple. And his kingdom and throne will never end."

So Nathan passed this message on to David – this kingly covenant promise that God wanted to make with him.

And David accepted that promise and gave God thanks for it.

And one day, far in the future, in the town of Bethlehem, from which David had come, a child was born.

A child descended from David. A child of promise. A child who had come to crush the serpent's head. And a child born to be a King – a King to reign for ever!

21. A WISE KING AND A KINGDOM DIVIDED
1 KINGS 3 v 1-28; 4 v 20 – 12 v 24

When King David died, his son Solomon inherited his throne. The kingly covenant promise that God had made with David passed on to Solomon, who was, at first, happy to be led by God.

One night, God visited him in a dream.

"What can I give you?" God asked.

"You showed my father your faithful love," Solomon replied. "And you have shown me that same love by giving me the throne. But I don't really know what I'm doing. I need your guidance to help me lead your people. So give me wisdom, that I might rule them well."

This was exactly the kind of answer God wanted to hear.

"You could have asked for riches," God replied. "Or a long life. Or to defeat your enemies. But because you have asked for wisdom, I will give you that and everything else too: wealth and honour and, if you continue to follow my commandments, a long life too."

Soon, Solomon's wisdom was put to the test.

Two women who lived in the same house were brought before him. Two women, and a baby.

"I had a baby," said the first woman. "And so did she. Her baby died though. And in the night, she swapped her dead baby for my living one. Make her give me my baby back!"

"Never happened," said the second woman. "That's my baby. Always has been."

"I see," said Solomon. "Guards, bring me a sword."

"You both say this is your baby. So I will cut the baby in two, and each of you can have half a baby."

The first woman fell to her knees. "Don't kill my baby," she begged. "Let him live and give him to this other woman."

But the second woman just shrugged. "Fine. Cut him in half. Then neither of us will have him."

At that moment, Solomon knew exactly who the real mother was.

"Give the baby to the first woman," he commanded. And when the people heard what had happened, they marvelled at his wisdom.

In fact, news of Solomon's wisdom spread all around the world, and visitors came from everywhere to meet him and to listen to the wonderful wise proverbs that he wrote.

More than that, Solomon fulfilled the dreams of David and built a magnificent temple for God, made of cedar wood and gold and stone. The ark of the covenant was brought inside – the box that held the two tablets upon which the Ten Commandments had been written. And, like a cloud, the presence of God filled that Holy Place.

When Solomon dedicated the temple to God, God appeared to him and told him that if he was faithful to the kingly covenant promise that God had made with David, his throne would last for ever. If, however, Solomon disobeyed God, his kingdom would crumble and the temple with it.

Sadly, Solomon was not faithful to God. He married women from many different nations and followed the gods of those nations too. And, sadder still, the very king who had built a temple for the true God ended up building places of worship for false gods.

So a man named Jeroboam rose up against Solomon and made a new nation called Israel out of the northern tribes, leaving only the tribes of Judah and Benjamin for Solomon's son, Rehoboam, to rule.

And a reign that started out so wise and so well finished up in ruins.

22. THE TRUE GOD
1 KINGS 16 v 29 – 17 v 1; 18 v 17-39

Jeroboam, the first king of Israel, in the north, was not related to Solomon and did not receive the promises God had made to David. So, while Judah, in the south, had a few good kings, Israel had no good kings at all!

Those kings ignored the kingly covenant promise that God had made in the time of Moses. They led his people in the worship of the gods of their neighbours – gods who were nothing more than statues made by human hands.

One of the worst was King Ahab. He angered God more than any of the kings who had come before him.

For a start, he married Jezebel, daughter of the king of Sidon. She worshipped a false god called Baal and encouraged Ahab to do the same. Then they insisted that God's people follow them.

So God sent his prophet Elijah to confront King Ahab, much as he had sent Moses to face Pharaoh many years before. Sadly, though, this was not a fight with a foreign king but a battle with the king of God's own people, who was determined to lead them away from him.

"Because of your disobedience, God will stop the rain," Elijah told Ahab. And just like Pharaoh, Ahab refused to change his ways.

For three long years, no rain fell. A famine followed. And when Elijah visited the king again, Ahab was furious.

"You have made nothing but trouble for Israel!" Ahab roared.

"I'm not the troublemaker," Elijah replied. "You are. You have broken the commandments of God and followed Baal instead. Invite the people to gather on Mount Carmel. Bring the prophets of Baal. We will have a contest. And we will see who is God and who is not."

When everyone had gathered, Elijah addressed the crowd…

"How long are you going to wander back and forth, from one god to another? If the Lord is God, follow him. Or follow Baal. Just choose!"

And then, like Moses before Pharaoh's magicians, Elijah addressed the 450 prophets of Baal.

"Kill a bull. Chop it into pieces. Set it on an altar. Then ask Baal to send fire from heaven and burn up the bull."

That's what the prophets of Baal did. They danced about and shouted and even cut themselves with their spears – all morning and into the afternoon. But no one answered. Because there was no one there!

Then Elijah took his turn. He built his altar out of twelve stones – one for each of the sons of Jacob. He dug a trench around it. And when he had placed the bull on the altar, he filled four large jars with water and poured the water over the bull and the wood and the stones. He did it again. And then again. Now the water filled the trench.

Then he prayed. "Show them that you are truly God," he asked. "And turn the hearts of your people back to you."

When the prayer was finished, fire fell from heaven! It burned up the bull and the wood and the stones and every drop of water in the trench!

When the people saw it, they fell on their faces and cried, "The Lord is God! The Lord is God!"

And God's people worshipped God their King once again.

23. ONE KINGDOM FALLS
2 KINGS 17 v 1-24; HOSEA 1 v 2; 11 v 1-7

When God's people had asked him for a king, he had warned them, hadn't he?

"Kings will take your fields. They'll turn your daughters into servants and your sons into soldiers." And, starting with Saul, so they had.

But when the kings disobeyed God and led his people in the worship of idols, that was even worse.

After Ahab died, the kings that followed him did just that. They turned the hearts of God's people against him. And even though God sent prophets like Elijah and Elisha to speak to his people and try to turn their hearts back, still they rejected him.

They built places to worship false gods on every hilltop in the land.

They made idols and called them gods, instead of following their true God and King.

They even burned up their own sons and daughters as sacrifices to those false gods.

And because they no longer worshipped and trusted God, they disobeyed the commandments that he had given to Moses and betrayed him in the way they treated one another as well.

God had made it plain in the kingly covenant promise he'd made to Moses.

If his people followed him and obeyed his commandments, they would receive his blessing and protection. But that's not what they were doing.

So, even though God loved them with an everlasting love, he decided to let them go.

It was hard. So hard, in fact, that the prophet Hosea compared God's heart to the broken heart of a man whose wife had left him.

And so, when the powerful nation of Assyria sent its army against Israel, it fell. Its people were carried off as slaves, never to return. In their place came people from many other countries, to make a new home in their land.

And the northern kingdom was a kingdom no more.

24. A FAITHFUL KING
2 KINGS 18 – 19

After the Assyrians had conquered the northern kingdom of Israel, they turned their attention and their mighty army towards Judah, in the south.

Unlike Israel, Judah had always been ruled by descendants of King David. Some of those kings disobeyed God. Some "sort of" obeyed him. But some reigned as good representatives of God and followed him faithfully.

Hezekiah was one of those. In fact, he was pretty much the exact opposite of bad kings like Ahab.

Bad kings worshipped false gods; Hezekiah worshipped the true God.

Bad kings built statues and places of worship to those gods; Hezekiah tore those places down.

Bad kings ignored God's commandments; Hezekiah followed them.

It was while Hezekiah was king that the powerful Assyrian army came marching into Judah.

The army had already captured the other walled cities in the land. And, given their strength, it looked as if the capital city, Jerusalem, would fall as well.

In those days, an army would surround a city so that the people inside couldn't get any fresh food. Then they would wait for them to starve or surrender.

That's what Sennacherib, king of the Assyrians, did with his army. And when he thought that Hezekiah was ready to give up, he sent his commander to talk to three of Hezekiah's men.

They met outside the city.

"Why don't you just surrender?" said the commander, using his very best Hebrew. "I hear you have made an alliance with Egypt. They're not going to help you. And as for your God, I don't care how many statues Hezekiah has torn down. Your God can't beat us either!"

"Could you speak in your own language, please?!" Hezekiah's men begged him. "Our people will hear what you're saying."

That was, of course, the commander's plan.

"Why shouldn't they hear the truth?" he shouted. In Hebrew. And even louder: "Their food is running out. Before long, they'll be drinking their own pee and eating their own poop!"

"But, if you give up," he shouted, louder still so everyone could hear, "you will live. And every one of you will have land and food and vineyards and water. We're the Assyrians! No one else's god has been able to stop us. And your God won't stop us either!"

That's not how King Hezekiah saw it though. He bowed his head before God.

"You are the Maker of heaven and earth," he prayed, "and Sennacherib worships gods made of wood and stone. Help us, please, and show the world that you alone are God."

It didn't take long. The prophet Isaiah sent Hezekiah a message from God.

"God says that our land will produce crops again," he told the king. "And we will eat what we have grown. As for Sennacherib, he will not enter this city or shoot an arrow within its walls. Instead, he will return to Assyria."

That night, God sent an angel to kill 185,000 Assyrian soldiers (much as he had done with the firstborn in Egypt). And then Sennacherib returned home, just as Isaiah had prophesied.

Hezekiah ruled for many more years. And the people of Judah did indeed live to plant their fields again.

25. PICTURES OF THE COMING KING
ISAIAH*

When God sent his prophets, their messages were sometimes about things that were happening at the time. But sometimes they were about things that would happen in the future.

And so it was that God gave Isaiah pictures of a future King, a servant King, a human King far more amazing than any king he'd met.

See if you can recognise him...

There was a picture of a young woman with a child called *Immanuel* – which means "God is with us".

There was a picture of mountains flattened and valleys lifted up and twisting roads made straight for the coming of God in all his glory. And a voice, crying out in the wilderness, "Prepare the way of the Lord!"

There was a picture of a light in the darkness, not just for God's people but for every nation.

There was a picture of a son – God's own gift – with names like Wonderful Counsellor, Mighty God, Everlasting Father and Prince of Peace.

There was a picture of David's throne – where this King would rule with righteousness and justice for ever.

There was a picture of a fresh shoot growing out of a tree stump – the stump of Jesse, David's father. So this King would be related to King David.

*Taken from Isaiah 7; 9; 11; 40; 42; 49; 50; 52; 53; 61

There was a picture of the poor and the meek, and the justice they would receive from the wisdom and understanding that God's Spirit would give this King.

There were pictures of wolves and leopards and lions and bears and cobras, living in peace with lambs and goats and calves and cows and children in the harmony this King would bring.

There were pictures of the poor getting good news, of broken hearts healed, of slaves set free, of the blind given sight. All because of this anointed one – God's Messiah,

And then there were pictures of the way that God would make this happen.

There was a bruised reed unbroken and a dimly burning candle – pictures of his gentleness and his quiet, persistent work to bring justice to the world.

But the cost to the King would be great.

So there were pictures of a back beaten, a beard pulled, and spit running down a face.

Not a beautiful face though. Instead a face so damaged that other kings stared in shocked silence at the state of it.

A face hated and rejected, marked by sorrow and grief. A face alone because everyone assumed that his punishment was from God.

Until they saw the next picture, that is, and realised what his suffering was for. For it was a picture of all of us. And all our grief and sorrow and sin healed by his wounds.

And then there were sheep. Sheep like us, wandering off in the wrong direction. And a lamb like him, led to slaughter, silently taking our sins upon himself, even though he had no sins of his own.

And finally, there was a picture of a rich man's grave. And the promise that God would honour him for his sacrifice and (somehow! surprise!) prolong his days.

That's the picture of the King. The Coming King. The Suffering King. The Servant King. The King that Isaiah saw!

26. THE REPENTANT KING
2 CHRONICLES 33 v 1-20

Hezekiah was one of Judah's best kings. But, sadly, his son Manasseh was one of the worst.

Idol by idol and sin by sin, Manasseh reversed all the good things his father had done.

He rebuilt the places where the false gods had been worshipped and filled them with brand new statues.

He worshipped those false gods, encouraged God's people to do the same, and even killed his own son as a sacrifice to them.

And as if that wasn't bad enough, he put an idol in the temple that Solomon had built as a dwelling place for the one true God.

God was not silent. He was, after all, the true King of his people. And he wasn't going to let their earthly king lead them in the wrong direction. So God sent his prophets – his spokesmen – to challenge the king.

But the king killed them, along with anyone else who objected to what he did. And the streets of Jerusalem ran red with blood.

So God acted. He allowed a foreign king – the king of Assyria – to capture Manasseh and drag him away in chains, with a hook through his nose. Ouch!

Sad and alone and in prison, Manasseh humbled himself before the God he had rejected, and begged for his help. He said he was sorry for all the awful things he had done.

And God heard his prayer.

And God forgave him.

And God brought him back to Jerusalem, where everything changed.

Manasseh tore down the altars to the false gods.

He removed the idol from God's holy temple.

And he threw that idol, along with all the others, into a dump outside the city walls.

And because of God's forgiveness, one of the worst kings that his people had ever had became a better king, by far.

27. THE KING WHO FOUND A BOOK
2 CHRONICLES 34 – 35

Josiah was only eight years old when he became king! His father, Amon, was not a good king at all. He led God's people in the worship of false gods and set up idols. But Josiah decided, even from a young age, to be different.

When he was only 16, he turned away from those false gods to worship the true God, who was the true King of his people. By the time he was 20, Josiah was tearing down the idols and destroying the places where they were worshipped. And when he was 26, he decided to repair the temple itself.

He told Hilkiah, the high priest, to take the money that people had given in the temple and use it to make those repairs.

As the carpenters and the masons sawed and chipped away, Hilkiah found a book. And not just any book – but the Book of the Law, which contained the commandments that God had given to Moses.

The book had obviously not been read for ages. So it's no surprise that some of Judah's kings had been able to lead God's people in the wrong direction.

That was not the case with Josiah though. When the book was read to him, he was so upset that he tore his clothes.

"Our fathers have not obeyed these commandments!" he cried. "God must be very angry with us. Go, find a prophet and let us hear what God has to say."

So Hilkiah and several other officials went to see Huldah, the prophetess.

"Yes, God is angry," she said, "and because his people have worshipped other gods, disaster will fall upon this place. As for Josiah, because he has humbled himself and repented, he will not live to see Jerusalem destroyed but will go to his grave in peace."

Josiah started work at once.

First, he called the people to gather at the temple. And everyone came – priests and prophets, men and women, the rich and the poor, the powerful and the weak. Then he read the Book of the Law to them all. And when he had finished, he made a promise to God that he would obey the commands in the book. And everyone agreed.

Then he tore down the statues of the false gods and wrecked the places where they were worshipped. It was a big job.

Finally, Josiah did something that had not been done for a very long time: he celebrated the Passover. That's right, the very feast that God himself had told his people to perform every year – the very feast designed to remind them of what he had done when he freed them from slavery – had been ignored for years.

No book! No celebration! No wonder God's people had been so easily deceived.

Still, there were Huldah's words and her warnings about the destruction of Jerusalem. And in the reigns of Josiah's sons and grandson, all of those words came true…

28. ANOTHER KINGDOM FALLS
JEREMIAH*

When God wanted his people to know what he thought about what they were doing, he would send his prophets to speak to them. And because God cared for his people – and was truly their King anyway – the prophets would speak God's truth to the earthly kings (who so often got things wrong).

Jeremiah was one of the prophets God chose to speak to Josiah and then to the sons who ruled after him: Jehoiakim and Zedekiah.

Jeremiah wasn't very old when God called him to be his prophet.

"But I'm just a youth," Jeremiah said.

And much as God had done when Moses made his excuses, he had an answer for that.

"I will be with you to save you. And the words you speak will be my words. Words that tear down and words that build back up again."

And so they proved to be.

Jehoiakim and Zedekiah did not follow the good path of their father, so when the Babylonian army invaded Judah, the words God gave Jeremiah were not words those kings wanted to hear...

"Because of what you have done, you will be conquered by Babylon and your people will be carried away into exile. Best to surrender now and save your people more suffering."

Jeremiah's words were often accompanied by creative actions. He buried his loincloth in dirt and then dug it up again to show the people that their sins had made them as useless as rotted underwear! He put a yoke, used to drive oxen, round his neck to show them how they would be led away by their enemies. He broke a jar to show them how their city would be broken.

In spite of this, however, the kings would not listen.

When Jeremiah wrote God's message on a scroll and sent it to Jehoiakim, the king had it read out, and after every three or four lines, he cut off that section with his knife and threw it in the fire!

Then Jeremiah's enemies even tried to have him killed. They dropped him in a cistern, and he would have died there, but God was true to his word. A man called Ebed-Melech came to Jeremiah's rescue and pulled him out.

In the end, Jeremiah's "tearing down" words came to pass. Jerusalem was conquered, the temple was destroyed, and the king and many of the people were carried away as captives to Babylon.

So what about those "building back up again" words?

Well, when Jerusalem was surrounded and no hope remained, God told Jeremiah to buy a field outside the city walls. It seemed to make no sense, but it was God's way of demonstrating that, after 70 years, a remnant of his people would return to their land, and fields would be bought and sold once again. It was message of hope, and not the only one.

"The time will come," said Jeremiah, "when God will make a new kingly covenant promise with his people, and he will forgive their sins and write his law on their hearts". And if that sounds like a covenant that stretched far beyond those people in that time and place, so it was.

For during their exile in Babylon, God would send more prophets. And they would speak of a coming King who would establish that covenant for ever.

*Taken from Jeremiah 1; 13; 19; 27; 32; 36; 38; 39

29. A NATION IN EXILE
DANIEL 1; 3; 6 – 7

No temple. No country. No king.

When the citizens of Judah were carried away to Babylon by their conquerors, they had to find a way to live a new life in exile.

The Babylonians didn't make it easy. They chose clever young men from noble families, educated them in their schools and taught them their ways. They wanted to turn them into good Babylonians in the hope that the rest of the exiled people would follow.

Daniel was one of those young men, along with his friends Hananiah, Mishael and Azariah. (You might know them better by their Babylonian names – Shadrach, Meshach and Abednego.)

Their problem was simple – how could they be faithful, in a foreign land, to the country and the king they'd lost and to the God whose temple had been destroyed?

The answer, as they discovered, could be complicated.

In the course of their education, they were offered meat that God said they should not eat. They wanted to obey and honour him, so they cleverly suggested a contest where they would eat only vegetables and the other young men would eat meat. When their diet proved healthier, they were chosen to serve both their God and their captors, and were given important jobs in the government.

When King Nebuchadnezzar commanded them to bow down before a huge statue, they knew that worshipping an idol would not please God. So they said, "No!" And when Nebuchadnezzar had them thrown into a fiery furnace, as punishment, God was in there, with them, to rescue them!

Many years later, when Babylon itself had been conquered by the Persians and Daniel was an old man, he had to decide between praying to God or obeying a law that said no one should pray to anyone but the king.

    Daniel chose God...

    ... and was thrown into a lions' den for his faithfulness. But God sent an angel to rescue him, and his enemies ended up in the lions' bellies instead.

God made Daniel a prophet and showed him some amazing visions of the times to come.

    In one vision, Daniel saw strange creatures come out of the sea. There was a lion with eagle's wings that turned into a man. There was a bear with three ribs between its teeth. There was a leopard with four wings and four heads. The last beast had chomping iron teeth and stamping feet and ten horns. And one little horn with eyes and a mouth.

    God told Daniel that these beasts were the earthly kingdoms to come.

    Then God showed Daniel a picture of himself – the "Ancient of Days" – with clothes white as snow and hair white as wool, sitting on a throne made of fire! And, finally, God told Daniel that in the days of that last beast, a "son of man" would come from heaven, and from him would come a kingdom that would never end.

    But how was that possible? A man – from heaven? Someone, somehow, who was both man and God?

    Daniel said that the vision upset him and made him turn pale. And it wasn't the only vision that a prophet would receive about a strange and amazing coming King...

30. A REMNANT RETURNS
EZRA 1 – 7; NEHEMIAH 1 – 9; ZECHARIAH 9 v 9; MALACHI 4 v 5-6

Seventy years. That's how long God's people lived in exile. Just as the prophet Jeremiah had predicted.

And during those 70 years, some pretty significant things happened in the land of their captors.

The Babylonians, who had destroyed Jerusalem and carried away her people, were themselves conquered by the Persians. And it was Cyrus, a Persian king, who was told by God to let the exiles return to their land.

King Cyrus not only sent them home; he also gave them the precious vessels that the Babylonians had taken from the Jerusalem temple – thousands of gold and silver bowls and basins!

The return didn't happen all at once. One group of exiles was followed by another, over something like a hundred years.

The first group was led by a man called Zerubbabel.

They settled in the land and rebuilt the temple, but it wasn't easy. In the time they had been away, other people had moved into their land. People who would later be called Samaritans.

Those people didn't like the idea of the temple being rebuilt, so they made trouble for the returning exiles. But that didn't stop the exiles returning.

The next group was led by a priest called Ezra. He taught God's laws to those who had returned and encouraged everyone to obey them.

Those Samaritans were still unhappy about the return of the exiles, and it became clear that the walls of Jerusalem would need to be rebuilt so that the people would have protection.

So word was sent to Nehemiah, cupbearer to the Persian king, Artaxerxes. He asked the king if he could go to Jerusalem and help his people rebuild the walls. And Artaxerxes not only agreed but sent the special wood to make that possible!

Under Nehemiah's leadership, the job was divided up among the many families that had returned. But it wasn't easy. With their enemies on the attack, the workmen were forced to build with a trowel in one hand and a sword in the other.

The walls and gates were still rebuilt in just 52 days, and the people celebrated by rededicating themselves to God.

So God was back in his temple. The people were back in their land. But there was no king.

So the prophets spoke of a coming King.

The prophet Zechariah, who had returned with the first group, told God's people to shout for joy because a King was coming who would be righteous and who would bring salvation to his people. And how would that King arrive? Humbly. And riding on a donkey!

(Does that sound like a King you know?)

Around the same time, the prophet Malachi also spoke to God's people. He looked far into the future and said that Elijah would return and he would announce the coming of the special promised King.

But after Malachi, there was nothing. Not a word from a prophet for 400 years. Until a man called John – a man who looked much like Elijah – stood on the banks of the Jordan River and announced that the King and his kingdom were about to arrive…

THE NEW TESTAMENT

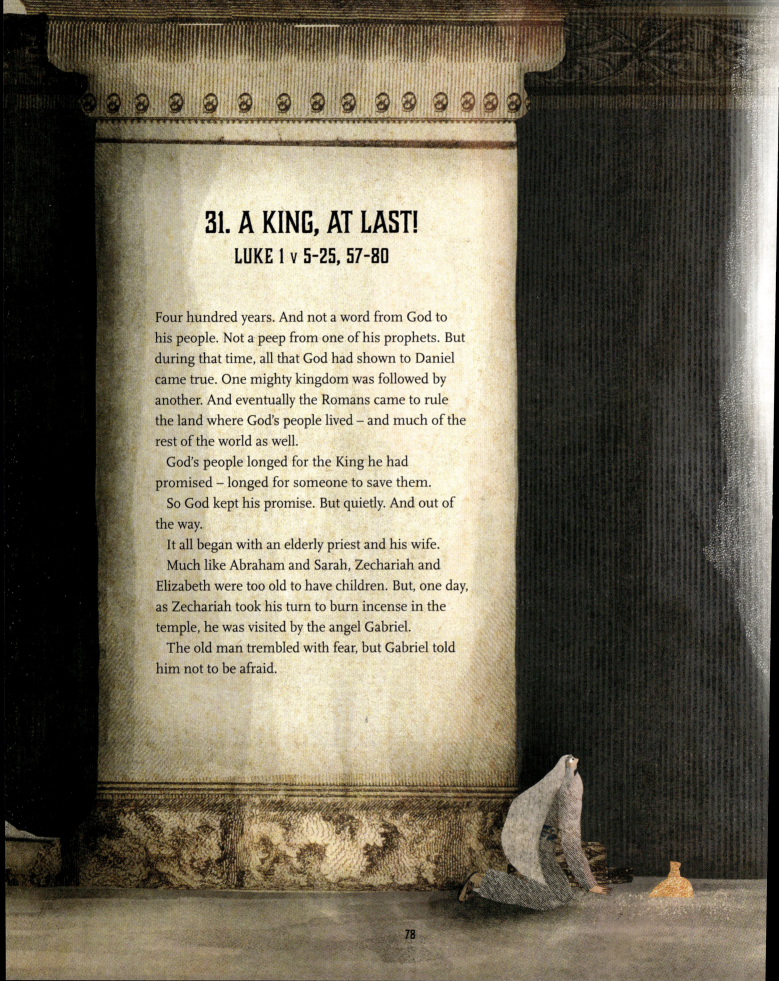

31. A KING, AT LAST!
LUKE 1 v 5-25, 57-80

Four hundred years. And not a word from God to his people. Not a peep from one of his prophets. But during that time, all that God had shown to Daniel came true. One mighty kingdom was followed by another. And eventually the Romans came to rule the land where God's people lived – and much of the rest of the world as well.

God's people longed for the King he had promised – longed for someone to save them.

So God kept his promise. But quietly. And out of the way.

It all began with an elderly priest and his wife.

Much like Abraham and Sarah, Zechariah and Elizabeth were too old to have children. But, one day, as Zechariah took his turn to burn incense in the temple, he was visited by the angel Gabriel.

The old man trembled with fear, but Gabriel told him not to be afraid.

"Your prayers have been heard," the angel assured him. "Your wife will have a son. You will call him John. And everyone will rejoice when he is born because God will use him to do great things. In fact, he will be filled with God's Spirit even while he is in his mother's womb!

"He will turn God's people back to him, just like Elijah." (It's what the prophet Malachi said, remember?)

"And he will prepare the way for the coming of the Lord, so his people will be ready to meet him." (Which is what the prophet Isaiah said!)

"But I'm an old man!" said Zechariah. "And my wife's an old woman. How do I know that what you say is true?"

"You don't believe me?" Gabriel replied. "Then here's the proof: you will not be able to speak until the time comes for you to name the child."

And, just like that, Zechariah could not say a word.

His time in the temple took much longer than usual, and everyone outside was worried. But when he appeared at last, all he could do was make signs with his hands to explain what had happened.

He went home, silent still. And couldn't even shout for joy when Elizabeth told him that she was pregnant.

Nine months later, when Elizabeth gave birth to a baby boy, everyone thought he would be given a family name. But Elizabeth said, "No, we will call him John".

So they turned to Zechariah. And when he wrote "John" on a clay tablet, suddenly he could speak again! In fact, he could hardly stop himself as he was filled with God's Spirit and told them all that John would, one day, do.

"He is part of God's plan to save us from our enemies," he explained. "Just as God promised to David and to Abraham."

And then Zechariah looked at the baby in his arms.

"You will be God's prophet, my child, and prepare the way for him. You will show everyone the path to salvation and forgiveness. And you will be there as his sun shines from on high and brings light and peace to all who sit in the darkness and the shadow of death."

And so John did, but not before an even more amazing child was born...

32. THE BIG ANNOUNCEMENT!
LUKE 1 v 26-56; MATTHEW 1 v 18-25

It was time! Ta-da! Time, at last! Time for the coming of God's long-promised King!

And so, in Nazareth, the angel Gabriel visited a young woman called Mary.

"Hello!" he said.

"You are blessed!" he said.

"Which means that God is with you and has set you apart for something very special!"

Mary didn't feel very special though. She was terrified, in fact, and tried to puzzle out what this blessing was about.

"Don't be afraid," the angel told her, much as he had done with Zechariah. "This is a good thing. God wants to do something wonderful for you. And here it is...

"You will have a son. You will call him Jesus. And he won't just be *your son*; he'll be *God's Son* too! God will sit him on David's throne, and he will rule over God's people for ever!"

Then Mary asked a puzzled question.

"How can I have a baby whose father is God?" she said. "How can that happen?"

And Gabriel had an amazing answer.

"God's Holy Spirit will come upon you. You will be wrapped in God's loving shadow. So the child will be holy – God's own Son.

"Look, your cousin Elizabeth, who could not have a child, is now six months' pregnant. Don't you see? Nothing is impossible for God!"

"Then I'll do it," Mary nodded. "I'll be God's servant."

And, with that, the angel left – and Mary journeyed all the way to Judah to visit her relative Elizabeth. She was very pregnant, just as Gabriel had said.

And when the two women met, the child in Elizabeth's womb leaped for joy, and now both mother and son were filled with God's Spirit!

"Blessed are you among women!" Elizabeth shouted. "And blessed is the child you are carrying! Blessed am I that the mother of my Lord should visit me. And blessed is the one who believes that God will keep his promise."

And, in reply, Mary sang a song of praise to God. Then she stayed with her relative for the next three months.

Someone else, meanwhile, had a hard decision to make.

An arrangement had been made for Mary to marry a man called Joseph. A man whose great-great-great- (and many "greats" more) grandfather was King David. When Joseph discovered that Mary was expecting a child, he knew the child was not his. He was a good man, though, and didn't want to shame her. So he decided to break off the marriage arrangement quietly.

That's when the angel came to him in a dream.

"Don't be afraid to make Mary your wife," the angel told him. "The child she is carrying really is from God. And when she gives birth to that son, you will call him Jesus – which means 'God saves' – for he comes to save his people from their sins."

It's what the prophet Isaiah had said would happen – remember? A young woman would give birth to a son, and he would be *Immanuel*, God with us!

So Joseph did as the angel said, and he married Mary.

33. A SUDDEN ANGEL SURPRISE
LUKE 2 v 1-20

During Mary's pregnancy, Caesar Augustus, the man who ruled Rome, decided that he wanted to see exactly how many people lived in his vast empire. So everyone had to go back to their home town to be counted.

Even though Joseph lived in Nazareth, up north, his home town was Bethlehem, down south. It's where King David was from, remember? And because Joseph was related to King David, that's where he was from too.

So Mary and Joseph set off for Bethlehem. It was an 80-mile journey.* A long way for anyone to walk, never mind someone who was going to have a baby. It's likely that they hoped to stay with some of Joseph's relatives. But by the time they got there, the lovely upper rooms, where relatives stayed when they visited, were already taken. So Mary and Joseph had to stay in another room, next to where the animals were kept.

And it was there, among the animals, that Mary gave birth to the Son of God, the promised King, the Messiah, the one who would sit on David's throne – to Jesus, whom she wrapped in cloths and laid in a manger.

*130 km

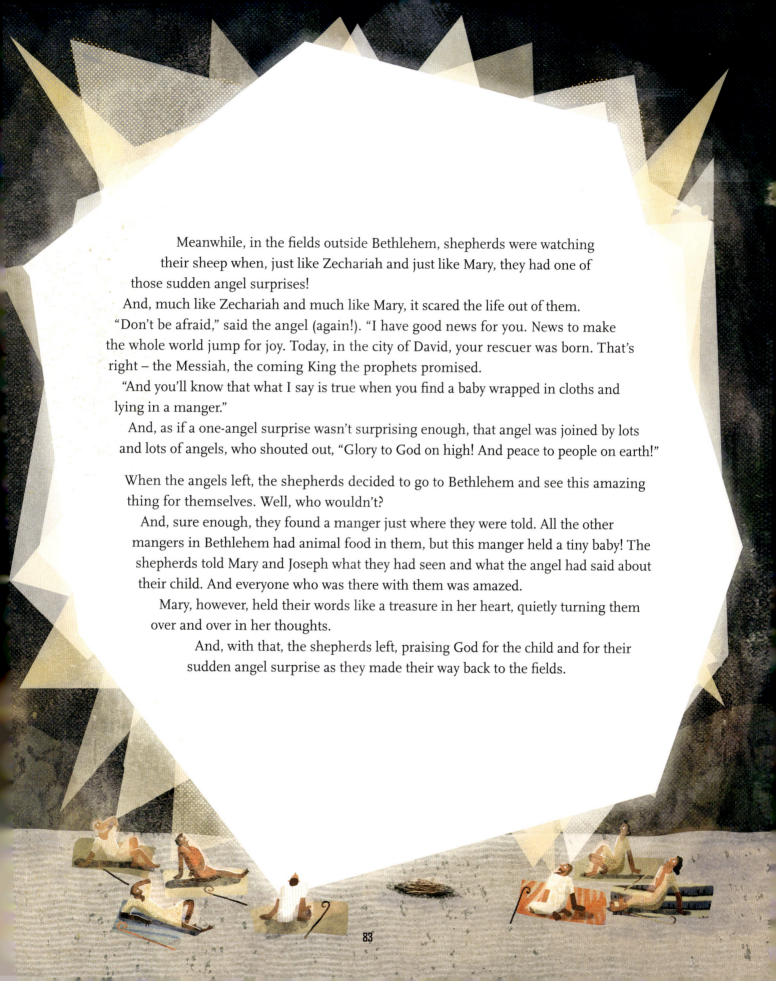

Meanwhile, in the fields outside Bethlehem, shepherds were watching their sheep when, just like Zechariah and just like Mary, they had one of those sudden angel surprises!

And, much like Zechariah and much like Mary, it scared the life out of them.

"Don't be afraid," said the angel (again!). "I have good news for you. News to make the whole world jump for joy. Today, in the city of David, your rescuer was born. That's right – the Messiah, the coming King the prophets promised.

"And you'll know that what I say is true when you find a baby wrapped in cloths and lying in a manger."

And, as if a one-angel surprise wasn't surprising enough, that angel was joined by lots and lots of angels, who shouted out, "Glory to God on high! And peace to people on earth!"

When the angels left, the shepherds decided to go to Bethlehem and see this amazing thing for themselves. Well, who wouldn't?

And, sure enough, they found a manger just where they were told. All the other mangers in Bethlehem had animal food in them, but this manger held a tiny baby! The shepherds told Mary and Joseph what they had seen and what the angel had said about their child. And everyone who was there with them was amazed.

Mary, however, held their words like a treasure in her heart, quietly turning them over and over in her thoughts.

And, with that, the shepherds left, praising God for the child and for their sudden angel surprise as they made their way back to the fields.

34. THE NEWS SPREADS
MATTHEW 2 v 1-15

"A king!" said the star-watcher. "A newborn king of the Jews! That's what the star is telling us."

And when the other star-watchers agreed, they set off west for Judea to worship him.

A king!

That's what Herod was. King of the Jews. He had to answer to Caesar, of course, seeing as the Romans had conquered his land. But he was still the local ruler of his people and very pleased with his position. So pleased, in fact, that he had murdered more than one of his relatives to keep it.

"A king!" the star-watchers explained, when they arrived, at last, at Herod's palace. "We're looking for a king. The newborn king of the Jews."

And so Herod left the star-watchers and gathered together the chief priests and other religious experts.

"A king?" he demanded to know. "What's all this about a king? Is it the coming King, the Messiah, they're going on about? And if so, where is this King supposed to be born?"

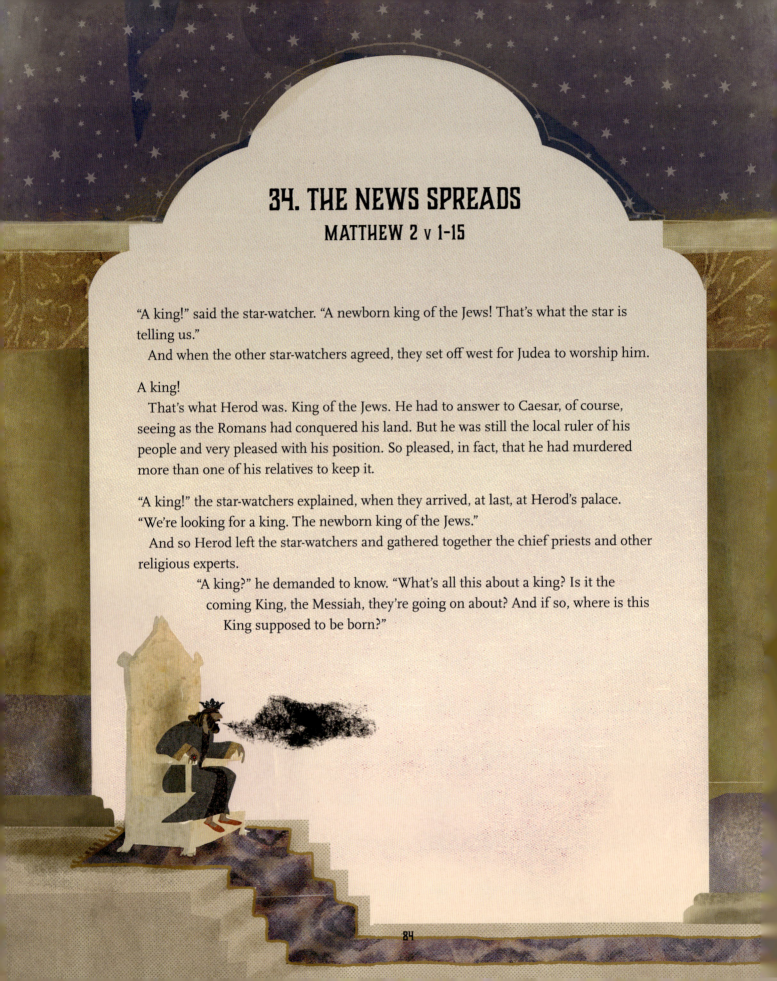

"The King," the chief priests told him, "is meant to be born in Bethlehem. That's what the prophet Micah said, many years ago – he said, 'from Bethlehem a ruler shall come who will be a shepherd to our people.'"

So Herod went back to the star-watchers.

"This king," he explained, "will be in Bethlehem. When you have found him, please come back and tell me, for I would like to worship him too."

"The king!" the star-watchers rejoiced, when the star had stopped finally above a house in Bethlehem. And when they went in and saw little Jesus and his mother, Mary, they fell down and worshipped him. And, as a part of their worship, they gave him gifts fit for a king – gold and frankincense and myrrh. But as they slept that night, they had a dream.

"Don't go back to Herod!" the dream revealed. "Do not return to his palace. Go home, instead, by another way."

So that's what the star-watchers did, while the newborn King and his family, led by another dream, fled to Egypt and stayed there until King Herod had died.

So the promised King survived. And, just as the prophets had promised, people other than God's chosen people, people from another part of the world entirely, came to know about...

The King!

35. TWO TEMPLE STORIES
LUKE 2 v 22-35, 41-52

Shortly after Jesus was born (and well before the star-watchers visited!), Mary and Joseph took him to the temple in Jerusalem.

God had killed the firstborn children of the Egyptians to free his people from slavery – remember? But he had spared the firstborn of his own people. So God told Moses that those firstborn belonged to him, and that his people would need to redeem them – to buy them back from him with a sacrifice – when they were born.

Jesus was Mary's firstborn child, so she and Joseph were there to make that sacrifice – with a pair of doves or pigeons.

While they were in the temple, they met a man called Simeon. God had promised Simeon that he would not die before he saw the Messiah, God's promised King. And when Simeon spotted baby Jesus, he knew he was the one! So he took the child in his arms and, thanking God, said, "Let me die in peace now, Lord. For I have seen with my own eyes the rescue you have prepared for the world: glory for your own people and a light for everyone else on earth!"

And then, quite solemnly, he told Mary that little Jesus would be responsible for the rise of many and the fall of many too. And that it would mean heartbreak for her as well.

Twelve years passed. And another visit to the temple gave Mary an idea of what that heartbreak might be like.

She and Joseph had taken young Jesus to Jerusalem to celebrate the Passover feast. It was a long walk – days, not hours! – and they were in the company of their friends and relatives. On the way home, after they had walked for a day, Mary and Joseph couldn't find Jesus. Worried, they asked everyone if they had seen him. No one had! So, even more worried, they walked for another day back to Jerusalem. For three days they searched through the city for Jesus. But still they could not find him. So, at last, they went to the temple.

And there he was!

But he wasn't just wandering about, lost. He was listening carefully and asking questions of the teachers.

"Your son is amazing!" they told Mary and Joseph. "He understands so much about what we believe!"

But Mary was more concerned about telling Jesus how worried they had been.

"Why have you treated us this way?" she said. "Your father and I were sick to death with worry! We've been looking everywhere for you!"

And Jesus' reply? Well, it wasn't an apology, that's for sure. More like an explanation.

"Why were you looking for me?" he asked.

"Didn't you know that this is where I would be? In the temple – in my Father's house?"

Mary and Joseph looked at each other, puzzled. They didn't know what to make of his answer. So, much as Mary had done with the shepherds' story, she held Jesus' answer like a treasure in her heart, quietly turning it over in her thoughts.

And back to Nazareth they all went, where Jesus grew up, obedient to them and in wisdom and in strength – a blessing to both God and people.

36. THE HERALD OF THE KING
MATTHEW 3 v 1-17; MARK 1 v 1-11; LUKE 3 v 1-22

A voice!

The prophet Isaiah had predicted that there would be a voice calling on God's people to prepare the way for his coming.

A voice!

The angel Gabriel told old Zechariah that his son John would be that voice.

A voice!

And when John grew up, he went out into the wilderness of Judea and raised his voice…

"God's kingdom is nearly here! You need to get ready for it. Tell God you're sorry for the wrong things you have done. And be baptised to show that you mean to turn your life around, and that you need the cleansing his kingdom will bring."

And, in response, people from Jerusalem and all over Judea went out into the wilderness to listen to him and to be baptised in the Jordan River.

The prophets of old had sometimes done some pretty unusual things. (Remember Jeremiah and his rotten underpants?) And John certainly looked the part. He wore a camel-hair coat and lunched on locusts and wild honey.

And he sounded like some of those old prophets too – unafraid to challenge what was wrong.

He told soldiers to stop threatening people.

He told tax collectors to take only what was owed to them.

And, just like those old prophets, he saved some of his harshest words for the religious leaders.

"You say you're descended from Abraham?" he said to them. "You think that will save you? Big deal! God can make children of Abraham from these stones on the ground.

"Snakes! That's what you really are! And the only thing that will save you is saying sorry for how wrongly you have acted and changing your ways. For God's axe is about to chop down every tree that does not bear good fruit!

"There is someone coming," he told them all. "Someone so mighty that I'm not even worthy to carry his sandals. And as for baptising – I do it with water, but he will baptise you with the Holy Spirit and fire!"

Then, sure enough, that *someone* came. For Jesus came from Galilee down to the Jordan River and asked John to baptise him.

"It should be the other way round," John protested. "You should be baptising me!"
"No," said Jesus. "This is the right thing for me to do."
So John gave in and baptised Jesus. And as soon as Jesus came up out of the water, the heavens opened, and the Holy Spirit came down and landed on him like a dove.
And with the Spirit came...
A voice!
The voice of God himself.

*"This is my much-loved Son.
And I am very pleased with him!"*

37. "IF YOU ARE THE KING..."
LUKE 4 v 1-13

After Jesus had been baptised, the Holy Spirit led him into the wilderness. He fasted – that is, he ate nothing – for 40 days and 40 nights.

Jesus was hungry. Jesus was tired. And that's when the devil, that old serpent, came to visit.

His lies had tricked Adam and Eve, all those years ago. They had introduced his rebellion to a world that God himself had made. So if he could trick the Son of God – the very one sent to crush the serpent's head – how great a victory that would be!

And so, much as he had done with Adam and Eve, the devil began the conversation with a discussion about food.

Well, food and lies.

"So you think you're the Son of God, do you?" said the devil, hoping to cast doubt even on that. "Well, *if* you are the Son of God, you don't need to be hungry anymore. You can turn that stone over there into a piece of bread."

Even though Jesus was hungry and even though he was tired, he was not so easily fooled. He knew a lie when he heard one. And he knew where to find the truth.

"Man does not live by bread alone," Jesus replied, "but by every word that comes from the mouth of God. That's what God himself says. It's written in our Scriptures."

So the devil tried another trick. Since Jesus had come to set up a kingdom, a kingdom is what he would offer him. He took Jesus up and showed him every kingdom of the world – in a moment, in a flash!

"These are all mine!" the devil said. "And they can be yours, too, if you will bow down and worship me."

It was another lie. Those kingdoms didn't belong to the devil. And Jesus knew it. More than that, he knew that God is the only one who deserves to be worshipped.

"You shall worship the Lord your God, and serve only him," Jesus answered. "That's what God himself says. It's written in our Scriptures."

The Scriptures! The Scriptures! The devil knew the Scriptures too. And he knew how to bend them to his own purpose. So he took Jesus to the top of the temple.

"Here is a Scripture for you," he said with a smile. "A Scripture all about God's chosen King."

Then, quoting from the Book of Psalms, he said...

"God will tell his angels to take care of you – to lift you up in their arms so you don't even stub your toe on a stone."

And then, smiling even more broadly, the devil continued.

"If you really are that chosen King, if you really are the Son of God, throw yourself down from the top of the temple. For God himself says that the angels will be there to catch you!"

"Here's another Scripture for you, then," Jesus replied. "Don't put God to the test!"

And with that, the devil stopped his test too. And left Jesus. And waited for a better time to tempt him.

38. THE KING WHO HEALS
MATTHEW 4 v 23-25; REVELATION 21 v 1-5

When Jesus left the wilderness, he returned to Galilee, up north. That's where he set to work.

From town to town he went, telling everyone, "The kingdom of God is near. Turn away from what's wrong and turn back to God."

But talking was not all that Jesus did. As he told people about the coming of God's kingdom, he also healed people. Lots and lots of people!

If people were paralysed, Jesus helped them to walk.

If people were blind, Jesus helped them to see.

If people were deaf, Jesus helped them to hear.

If people were troubled by evil spirits, Jesus chased those spirits out.

And if people were hurting, Jesus took away their pain.

It's no surprise, then, that crowds came from all over Galilee and beyond, bringing their sick friends and family to be healed by Jesus.

But why did Jesus do the two together – healing people and telling them about the coming of God's kingdom?

It's because, as well as caring for people and helping them, Jesus wanted everyone to know that when he is King, things that are wrong are put right.

Way back in the beginning, when God made that beautiful garden for Adam and Eve, there was no death because there was no illness. It was only when Adam and Eve ate the fruit and joined the serpent's rebellion that death came into the world.

What's more, prophets like Isaiah had made it very clear that healing would be a part of what the Messiah, God's chosen one, would do when he came. Do you remember – Isaiah said that the blind would be given sight?

And then there was the future. For, as Jesus would one day show his friend John, when God makes his new heaven and new earth for us to enjoy for ever – when his kingdom finally comes in all its fullness – there won't be any suffering or pain or tears there either. For everything broken will be made new again!

So healing people was a clear and obvious sign that Jesus really had come from God, that God's kingdom was truly near, and that Jesus was the one he had chosen to build it.

But not everyone believed that Jesus was the one...

39. HOME-TOWN BOY
LUKE 4 v 14-30

Jesus' tour of Galilee was quite a sensation. In each town he visited, he taught in the synagogue, and all the people loved what he said and were amazed by him. So when he came to his home town, Nazareth, he went to the local synagogue as usual.

It was the normal custom to ask visiting teachers – rabbis, as they were called – to read the Scriptures and comment on them. So Jesus was handed a scroll which contained the words of the prophet Isaiah.

Jesus unrolled the scroll until he reached one of those prophecies that Isaiah had written to show people a picture of the Messiah – do you remember?

It was the one about the poor receiving good news, about broken hearts being healed, about slaves being set free, and about the blind being given sight – a picture of some of the things that would happen when God's kingdom arrived.

When Jesus had finished reading the passage, he simply told the crowd, "This Scripture is coming true, today, as you hear it!"

At first, everyone was amazed by Jesus' words. But when they had thought about it for a moment, they said, "Hang on, isn't this Joseph's son?" As if someone like the Messiah couldn't possibly come from their town.

"I know what you're thinking," said Jesus. "Why don't I do the miracles here that I have done in other parts of Galilee – like Capernaum?

"The thing is that, when they're in their home town, when people think they know them, prophets tend not to be welcomed.

"Back in Elijah's day, there were plenty of widows in Israel – in his homeland – who needed help. But God sent him to help a widow from Sidon – a foreigner.

"And in the time of Elisha, whom did God heal of leprosy? That's right, Naaman, the Syrian. Another foreigner!"

Now maybe it was the fact that Jesus wasn't doing any miracles for them. Or maybe it had to do with his suggestion that God's servants – including his Messiah – were interested in helping foreigners too. Whatever the reason, the crowd turned on Jesus and drove him out of town to the top of the cliff upon which Nazareth was built. Then they tried to throw him over the edge!

But Jesus simply walked through the crowd and left. And the home-town boy said goodbye to his home town and made his way to the other towns in Galilee.

40. DISCIPLES OF THE KING
LUKE 5 v 1-11; JOHN 1 v 43-51

It was the custom for teachers like Jesus to choose disciples, whom they would teach and train in their ways.

And while Jesus did that too, the way he chose his disciples was sometimes very different from other teachers – and was designed to show his disciples, right from the start, who he really was.

Jesus was teaching on the shore of Lake Galilee. And the crowd that came to hear him was huge. He needed to back away a bit so that he could be seen and heard by everyone. And that's when he spotted a couple of fishing boats.

He asked Simon, one of the fishermen, if he could borrow one of the boats. So Simon rowed him out a little way from the beach, and from there, Jesus taught the crowd.

When he had finished teaching, Jesus said to Simon...

"Let's go out into the deep water and catch some fish."

"We were out all night!" Simon replied. "And caught nothing. But if you say so, sir, we'll have a go."

So out they went. And as soon as Simon dropped his nets into the water, they were filled with fish. Loads and loads of fish. So many fish, in fact, that the nets began to break!

Simon called out to his friends James and John to come and lend a hand. And, even then, there were so many fish in both boats that they looked like they would sink.

When he saw the huge catch of fish, Simon fell to his knees before Jesus and cried out, "Go away, please, for I'm a sinful man, Lord". (Which is pretty much the kind of thing people said when they recognised that God was at work.)

"Don't be afraid," Jesus replied. "From now on, you'll be fishing for men!"

And when they returned to the beach, Simon and his brother Andrew and their friends, James and John, left everything to follow Jesus.

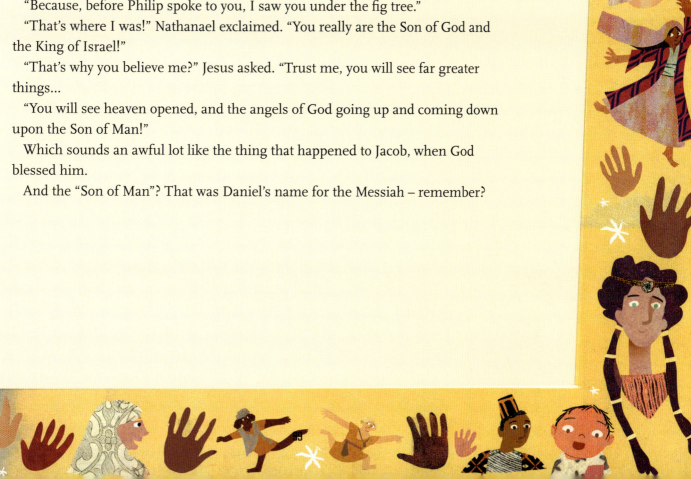

Simon (also known as Simon Peter) and Andrew came from Bethsaida. So Jesus went there and asked a man called Philip to follow him too. And Philip went to find his friend Nathanael.

"He's the one we've been waiting for!" Philip told his friend. "The one that Moses and the prophets wrote about. His name is Jesus. He's from Nazareth."

"Nazareth?" Nathanael sneered. "Has anything good ever come from Nazareth?"

"See for yourself," Philip replied. And when they found Jesus, Jesus looked at Nathanael and said...

"Here comes a true Israelite – a man who says exactly what he thinks!"

"How do you know me?" asked Nathanael.

"Because, before Philip spoke to you, I saw you under the fig tree."

"That's where I was!" Nathanael exclaimed. "You really are the Son of God and the King of Israel!"

"That's why you believe me?" Jesus asked. "Trust me, you will see far greater things...

"You will see heaven opened, and the angels of God going up and coming down upon the Son of Man!"

Which sounds an awful lot like the thing that happened to Jacob, when God blessed him.

And the "Son of Man"? That was Daniel's name for the Messiah – remember?

41. JESUS, KING OF CREATION
LUKE 8 v 22-25

Jesus didn't just talk about the kingdom of God. Time and time again, Jesus showed his disciples exactly what it meant for him to be the King.

One day, they were all in a boat, splashing along the shore of Lake Galilee, when Jesus said, "Let's sail across to the other side".

He was their master. They were his disciples. So they did what disciples do, and followed him.

It had been a long day. Jesus had been teaching the crowds, and he was tired. So he curled up on a cushion at the back of the boat and fell asleep.

Quietly, peacefully, the boat slipped across the calm waters. Everything was lovely.

Until it wasn't!

Out of nowhere, a storm blew up around them. The wind howled – the waves churned. And before long those waves washed their way into the boat, filling it and threatening to drag it to the bottom of the lake.

The disciples were terrified. But Jesus? Jesus was still asleep in the back.

So together they shouted, "Master, we're going to die!"

And when Jesus had woken up, and sat up, he looked up at the black skies and shouted, "That's enough, now! Quiet!"

Then he looked round at the pounding waves and told them off as well. "Calm down, do you hear me? Now!"

And as soon as he'd said it, the day was peaceful and the waters quiet, once again.

"Why didn't you trust me?" he asked his disciples.

And no one dared answer, for they had a question of their own.

"Who is Jesus? Who is he really, when even the wind and the waves do exactly what he says?"

But we know, don't we? Because we remember, way back in the beginning, when a voice spoke and the waters moved at his command.

Who is Jesus? He's the King of all creation!

42. JESUS, KING OF THE SABBATH
MATTHEW 12 v 1-14

When Jesus stopped that terrifying storm, it showed the disciples that Jesus really was the King of creation. But he wanted to show them that he was King of so much more.

On one Sabbath day, they were walking through a field of corn.

The Sabbath was the day set aside for rest. It was one of the ten commandments that God had given to Moses – remember? And it was a reminder and a celebration of the fact that God himself had rested when he had finished creating the world.

As Jesus and his disciples walked along, his disciples plucked and ate bits of corn from the field.

"Hang on!" said some Pharisees – religious leaders who were very keen to stick strictly to God's law. "Work is not allowed on the Sabbath. And plucking corn and eating it is work!"

But Jesus had an answer for them, from the life of King David, to whom he was related – remember?

"Have you not read," Jesus began (which sounded an awful lot like the beginning of the answers he had given to the tempter – hmmm), "when David was hungry, he and his men ate bread from the tabernacle, which the law said should only be eaten by the priests?"
In other words, if it was okay for David to meet a need by breaking the law, why shouldn't it be okay for Jesus? He was, after all, the heir to David's throne!

And then Jesus said something else, even more amazing.

"The Son of Man is King of the Sabbath."

There it was again – the Son of Man – Daniel's name for the Messiah. But there was more…

Since God had made the Sabbath and Jesus was "God with us", then surely it was up to him to say what was right and what was wrong to do on that day.

And that's what Jesus did, when he and his disciples went from the fields to a synagogue.

There was a man in that synagogue who had a hand so bent and twisted that he could not use it.

So the religious leaders asked Jesus, "Isn't it against our law to heal someone on the Sabbath?"

And, again, Jesus had an answer for them.

"If any of you had a sheep that had fallen into a pit, you'd pull it out, wouldn't you? Even if it was the Sabbath.

"Well, how much more valuable is a man than a sheep? There is nothing in our laws that says it is wrong to help someone on the Sabbath."

And with that, Jesus told the man to stretch out his hand. And there was no longer anything wrong with it. The man was healed!

The religious leaders, however, were furious. And they decided that Jesus – the one that God had sent – was a danger to them and had to be destroyed.

43. JESUS, KING OF ALL
MATTHEW 8 v 5-13

"Help me, Jesus!" the centurion cried. "My servant is suffering. He's lying at home and can't move. Will you heal him, please?"

Now, this centurion was not Jewish. Not at all.

He was a Roman. And more than that, he was a commander in the Roman army that occupied the land God had given his people.

It was true that he had been as kind as possible to the people of the town where he was based. He had even built them a synagogue. But he was still, officially, the enemy.

So what would Jesus do?

"I will come to your house. I will heal your servant," Jesus answered.

That's what he would do.

"But I am not worthy to have someone like you under my roof," the centurion replied. "Just say the word, and I know my servant will be healed.

Just like you, I know what it means to be in charge. I'm an officer in the army. If I order a soldier to go, he goes. If I order him to come, he comes. And if I tell my servant to do something, he does it."

Jesus was amazed.

"Listen up!" he said to everyone gathered around him. "This man has shown more faith in me than any of our own people. I want you to understand this: people from all over the world – from the east and from the west – will be welcomed at the table and eat with Abraham, Isaac and Jacob in the kingdom of heaven.

"But some of our own people – from the family that God gave to Abraham – will miss out on the kingdom altogether."

It's what God promised Abraham, remember? That his nation would be a blessing to the whole world.

And it's what the prophet Isaiah said as well – that the Messiah would be a light to every land.

And so Jesus said to the centurion, "Go! The thing you believed would happen will happen indeed."

And at that very moment, his servant was healed!

44. JESUS, THE KING WHO CONQUERS EVIL SPIRITS

LUKE 11 v 14-22

The man could not speak.

Not a sound. Not a whisper. Not a word.

And the reason? The man was controlled by an evil spirit – which means a servant of that serpent, the devil, who had tempted Jesus in the wilderness.

Jesus had shown his power over the devil at that time, and because he wanted to help the man who could not speak, he was determined to show his power again.

So when Jesus told the evil spirit to leave the man, that's exactly what the evil spirit did. And, just like that, the man could speak.

Sounds and whispers and words and all!

Most of the people who witnessed this were amazed. But some, sadly, were suspicious.

"He used the devil's own power to cast out that evil spirit!" they suggested.

And, just as he'd had answers for the devil, Jesus had answers for them as well.

"If a kingdom is divided and fights against itself, it will fall," he said.

"The same is true for a family. So why would the devil drive out an evil spirit and fight against himself?

"You say that I used the devil's powers to cast out this evil spirit. But you pray for people to be released from evil spirits as well. Whose powers do *you* use?

"If, however, it was by the powerful finger of God that I drove out this evil spirit, then God's kingdom has truly arrived!

"Look at it this way: a strong man can arm himself and do everything he can to guard his palace. But when someone stronger arrives, he will take that strong man's armour and defeat him. Then he will take everything the strong man thought belonged to him."

And that's exactly what happened on that day. The evil spirit had taken the man's voice. He thought it belonged to him. But Jesus was the stronger man, who took back the voice and gave it to its true owner.

Sounds and words and whispers and all!

45. A KINGDOM OF KIDS AND CAMELS
LUKE 18 v 15-27

Jesus' miracles weren't just amazing; they also pointed to the coming of the kingdom of God.

But what was life in this kingdom meant to be like? That is what Jesus made clear, through the lessons he taught, the parables he told and the way he lived.

It was, for a start, a kingdom full of surprises! A kingdom meant to challenge and change the way that people looked at God and at each other. And to take them back to the way that God, the loving King, intended the world to work, right from when he created it.

Take children, for example. In Jesus' time, children weren't valued nearly as much as grown-ups. But that wasn't the way God made things to be.

One day, some parents brought their children to see Jesus. They even brought little babies. They wanted Jesus to place his hands on the children and pray for them. But when the disciples saw the children, they were cross with the parents and told them to take their children away.

Jesus was very unhappy with his disciples.

"Let the children come to me!" he insisted. "Don't keep them away. You need to receive the kingdom of God like a child if you want to get in."

And in that way, Jesus not only showed how important children were but also how important it was for everyone to be like children and to trust God and depend on him for what they needed.

And maybe that's why the disciples were surprised, once again, when a rich man came to see Jesus.

In Jesus' day, rich men were the opposite of children. People thought the rich were very important indeed, and specially blessed by God because of their wealth. But, again, that wasn't the way God made things to be.

"What can I do to live with God for ever?" the rich man asked Jesus.

"You know the commandments," Jesus replied. "Be faithful to the person you marry. Don't murder. Don't steal. Don't lie. And honour your father and your mother."

"I have kept all of these since I was young," replied the rich man.

"Then there's just one more thing you need to do," said Jesus. "Sell everything you have and give it to the poor. That way, the only treasure you have left will be in heaven. And when you have done that, come and follow me."

The man looked very sad, for he wasn't just rich; he was very rich indeed.

And when Jesus saw his sadness, he said, "It's very hard for a rich man to enter the kingdom of God. In fact, it's easier for a camel to squeeze through the eye of a needle!"

The disciples were shocked. For, as with the children, they were still stuck in their old way of looking at the world.

"If a rich man can't be saved," they said, "what hope is there for the rest of us?"

"God can do what people find impossible!" Jesus replied.

And this was just one of many times that he helped his disciples to see things in a brand new, old-as-creation way!

46. A KINGDOM OF SECOND (AND MANY MORE!) CHANCES
MATTHEW 18 v 21-35

Jesus never stopped surprising his disciples as, time after time, he showed them what life in God's kingdom was all about.

One day, Peter asked him how often he should forgive someone who had hurt him but then said they were sorry.

"Seven times?" suggested Peter, which surely seemed generous to him. But Jesus had another surprise up his sleeve.

"Not seven times," he said. "But 70 times seven!"

And yes, if you do the sums, that's 490 times. But it's likely that what Jesus was really saying was "as many times as necessary". Which he made clear in the parable he went on to tell Peter…

"This is what the kingdom of heaven is like.

"There was once a king who decided to deal with the servants who owed him money. When he looked at his account books, he discovered that one of his servants owed him 10,000 talents."

(Now, this was not a little sum. And this was not a middling sum. This was an enormous, gigantic sum – about 20 years' wages – that the servant had no hope of ever paying back!)

"So the king ordered his men to sell this servant and his wife and his children as slaves, and to take everything the man owned.

"The servant fell on his knees before the king and begged him for more time.

"'I'll pay back everything I owe!' he promised (which was, of course, impossible).

"What did the king do? He felt sorry for the man. He set the man free. And more than that, he forgave the man's debt. That's right, he told the servant that he no longer owed him anything!

"On his way home, this servant bumped into another servant – a man who owed money to him."

(Not an enormous, gigantic sum. Not a middling sum. Hardly a little sum, even. Just a tiny, itty-bitty sum.)

"And what did the servant do? Did he feel sorry for the man who owed him money? Did he forgive his debt, as his own debt had been forgiven?

"He did not.

"He grabbed the man by the throat and choked him.

"'Pay me what you owe me!' he demanded.

"And even though the man fell to his knees and begged for more time, just as he had done, that made no difference to the first servant. And he had the man thrown into jail until his debt could be paid.

"The rest of the king's servants were very upset by this. And when they told the king what had happened, he was upset too.

"'You evil man!' he cried. 'You begged for mercy, and I forgave your debt. Shouldn't you have shown the same mercy to your fellow servant?'

"And, with that, he had the man thrown into prison until his debt could be paid.

"And that," Jesus said to Peter, finally, "is how my Father in heaven will treat you if you don't forgive from the depths of your heart anyone who is sorry for hurting you and asks for forgiveness".

47. A KINGDOM OF SERVANTS
MARK 10 v 35-45

Jesus was always ready to surprise his disciples whenever the matter of God's kingdom came up.

One day, James and John approached him with a question.

"Teacher," they asked, "will you give us whatever we want?"

"It depends on what you want," Jesus replied.

"Well," they grinned, "when you finally show everyone that you're the King, could one of us rule with you on your right-hand side and the other rule with you on your left?"

Now, Jesus knew what they didn't know – that being the King God had promised to send, and showing everybody what that meant, would mean dying on a cross and, as Isaiah said, healing the wounds of the world with his own wounds.

So Jesus said to them, "You don't realise what you're asking for. Can you drink the cup I'm going to drink or be baptised with the baptism I must face?"

Which was simply Jesus' way of saying, "Can you go through the things I must go through?"

"Of course we can!" they nodded innocently.

"And so you shall," Jesus nodded. "But to decide who sits at my right hand and at my left is not my choice to make. Those places have already been prepared."

And that should have been that.

But when the other ten disciples heard of this conversation, they were really angry with James and John for asking for this in the first place.

So Jesus called them all together.

"Listen," he said. "The rulers of this world get their way by pushing people around. But that's not how I want you to act. In God's kingdom, your greatness will be shown by the way you serve each other. And the first among you will be the one who is willing to be the slave of all!

"And why is that? Because the Son of Man did not come to be served. That's right. I came to be a servant, and to give up my life as the price that sets people free from sin and death!"

The disciples still didn't get it, sadly. But the time was coming when they would understand exactly what Jesus was talking about.

48. A KINGDOM OF THE LOST AND FOUND
LUKE 15 v 1-32

It wasn't just Jesus' disciples who were surprised by what he taught them about God's kingdom. He surprised the religious leaders too.

They mostly hung out with people like themselves. But Jesus often ate with people who had done bad things.

"Why do you spend time with *them*?" the religious leaders asked him. And Jesus answered them with three parables.

"Let's say that one of you has a hundred sheep," he began. "And one of them wanders away. Wouldn't you leave the 99 other sheep and search for that lost sheep until you found it? Of course you would!

"Then you'd take it home, and tell your neighbours and friends, and celebrate, wouldn't you? Because the sheep that had been lost was found.

"In the same way, there is more joy in heaven over someone who turns away from the wrong things they have done and turns back to God than there is over 99 people who don't need to turn their lives around.

"Now, let's say there was a woman who lost one of her ten silver coins. Wouldn't she do everything she could to find it? Of course she would!

"She'd light a lamp, and sweep the house, and search everywhere until she found it. And when she did, she'd say to her neighbours and friends, 'Rejoice with me. My coin was lost, and now it's found!'

"And rejoicing is what the angels do when someone who hasn't been living for God turns around and starts living for him."

And, finally, Jesus said...

"There was a man who had two sons. The younger son asked his father to give him the share of the property he would inherit when his father died.

"The father divided what he owned between the two sons. And, almost immediately, the younger son set off for a country far away.

"And there he spent all that money, doing some very bad things.

"When the money was gone, that country was struck by a famine. So the young man took a job feeding pigs. And he was so hungry that he would gladly have eaten the pig food! No one helped him though.

"And then, one day, he came to his senses.

"'My father's servants are better off than this,' he sighed. 'I'll return to my father, admit that I was wrong, and ask to be one of those servants. For I'm no longer worthy to be his son.'

"But when the father saw him coming, he ran to greet his long-lost son.

"He hugged him and kissed him and called for his servants to bring a robe and a ring and a pair of shoes for the young man. Then he told them to kill his finest calf and throw a party.

"When the older son discovered this, he was furious.

"'I have served you faithfully for years!' he complained to his father. 'And you have never even served me a goat! But this son of yours does awful things with your money, and you welcome him back with your finest calf!'

"'All I have is yours,' the father replied. 'And you are always with me. But it's right for us to celebrate. For your brother was dead, and now he's alive! He was lost, and now he's found!'"

49. A KINGDOM OF EDGES AND HEDGES
LUKE 14 v 12-24

Jesus was invited to a banquet. And while he was eating, he made a surprising suggestion to his host.

"The next time you have a feast," Jesus said, "why not change the guest list? Instead of inviting your friends or your relatives or your rich neighbours, make room around your table for the poor, the lame, the crippled and the blind. They won't be able to repay you by inviting you back. But you will be repaid when God raises from the dead those who believe and trust in him."

When he heard that, one of the other guests said, "Blessed is everyone who will eat bread in God's kingdom!"

So Jesus told them all a God's-kingdom banquet story...

"There once was a man who decided to host a great banquet. When everything was prepared, he sent his servant round to those he had invited.

"'Come to the banquet!' the servant said. 'Everything is ready.'

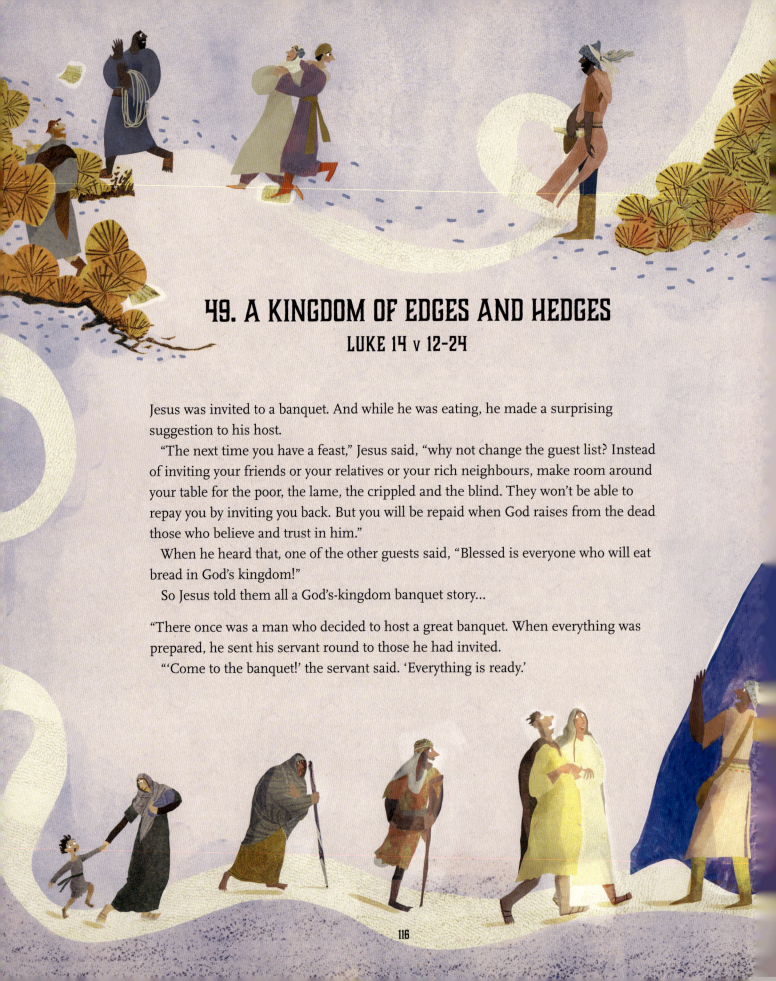

"'Sorry. Can't come,' said one of the guests. 'Just bought a field. Need to check it out.'

"'Can't come either,' said a second guest. 'There are five new pairs of oxen I need to test.'

"'Just married!' said a third guest. 'Sorry.'

"When the servant shared these excuses with his master, the master was very angry.

"'Then go into the city,' he said. 'Search up and down the streets and alleys. Invite the poor, the lame, the crippled and the blind you find there.'

"So that's what the servant did. But when they had all arrived, there was still room at the table.

"So the master said, 'Go out beyond the edges of the city – to the highways and the hedges – and tell the people you find there that they must come as well. I want my house to be full!'

"'And as for those who made excuses,' the master said, 'not one of them will taste my banquet food!'"

50. A KINGDOM OF UNLIKELY NEIGHBOURS
LUKE 10 v 25-37

The religious leaders never stopped trying to trip up Jesus. And every time they did, he used it as an opportunity to teach them something new about God's kingdom.

One day, a man who was an expert in the laws that God had given his people asked Jesus a question. It wasn't an honest question. The man was simply trying to see if Jesus would give the "right" answer.

"Teacher," the man said, "what do I need to do to live for ever with God?"

Jesus knew what the man was up to, so he answered with a question or two of his own.

"What does God's law say about that?" he replied. "How do you understand it?"

"Love the Lord your God with all your heart and soul and strength and mind," the man answered, quoting from the Old Testament book of Deuteronomy. "And love your neighbour as you love yourself."

"That's right," Jesus agreed. "Do that and you will, indeed, live for ever with God."

But the man didn't stop there. He was still keen to see if Jesus thought about things the same way he did. And that's why he asked a follow-up question.

"So who is my neighbour, then?"

And Jesus answered with a story...

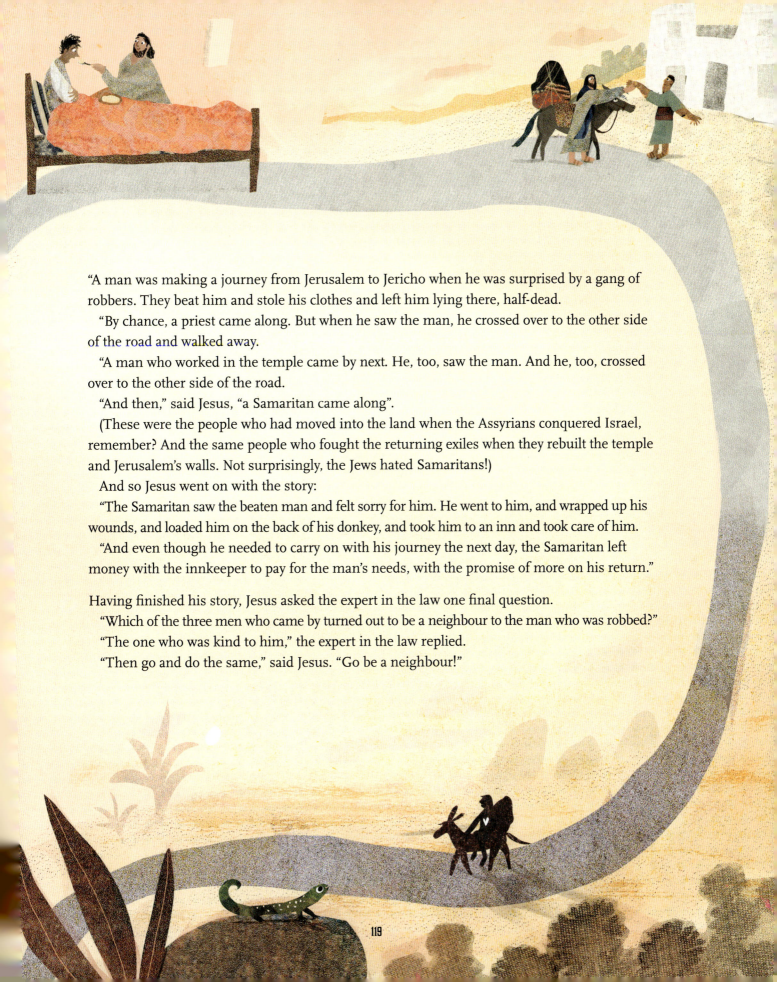

"A man was making a journey from Jerusalem to Jericho when he was surprised by a gang of robbers. They beat him and stole his clothes and left him lying there, half-dead.

"By chance, a priest came along. But when he saw the man, he crossed over to the other side of the road and walked away.

"A man who worked in the temple came by next. He, too, saw the man. And he, too, crossed over to the other side of the road.

"And then," said Jesus, "a Samaritan came along".

(These were the people who had moved into the land when the Assyrians conquered Israel, remember? And the same people who fought the returning exiles when they rebuilt the temple and Jerusalem's walls. Not surprisingly, the Jews hated Samaritans!)

And so Jesus went on with the story:

"The Samaritan saw the beaten man and felt sorry for him. He went to him, and wrapped up his wounds, and loaded him on the back of his donkey, and took him to an inn and took care of him.

"And even though he needed to carry on with his journey the next day, the Samaritan left money with the innkeeper to pay for the man's needs, with the promise of more on his return."

Having finished his story, Jesus asked the expert in the law one final question.

"Which of the three men who came by turned out to be a neighbour to the man who was robbed?"

"The one who was kind to him," the expert in the law replied.

"Then go and do the same," said Jesus. "Go be a neighbour!"

51. PICTURES OF THE KINGDOM
MATTHEW 5 v 1-48

The prophets Isaiah and Jeremiah used word pictures when they talked about God – remember?

Jesus did the same thing when he described what it meant to live in God's kingdom. And like the prophets' pictures, the word pictures Jesus drew surprised the people who heard them. They thought that God's kingdom was all about beating their enemies and being "winners". But Jesus' pictures were about those whom some people might have called "losers"!

First, there were pictures of people on their knees, hurting and desperate, with arms reaching out to God for help. So Jesus called them "blessed", because that need would draw them closer to him.

"Blessed are those who feel empty inside, as if something is missing," Jesus said. "The kingdom of God is theirs.

"Blessed are those who cry out in pain for what they have lost, for they will receive comfort.

Blessed are the meek and humble – who don't make a big deal of themselves. They will inherit the earth!

Blessed are those who are hungry for all that is good. God will fill them up full!

Blessed are those who show mercy, for they will receive mercy.

Blessed are those whose hearts are pure. They will see God!

Blessed are those who make peace. They will be called God's children.

Blessed are those who are hurt for doing good and living my way. The kingdom of heaven is theirs.

"And if people hurt you because you follow me," said Jesus, "or tell lies about you, then you are blessed too. Because that's exactly what happened to the prophets." Then there were pictures of salt and light, because living the kingdom life would bring flavour and brightness to the world. "You are like a glowing city on a hill," said Jesus. "So shine!"

There was a picture of a heart as well.

Jesus said that he did not come to get rid of the law, but that living in God's kingdom was more than just obeying rules. It had to do with what went on inside someone's heart (which is what the prophet Jeremiah promised, remember? – when he said that the heart was where God would one day write his law!).

So murder starts in the heart – with anger and hatred and refusing to patch up differences.

And being disloyal to your husband or wife starts in the heart too – with wanting someone else.

And the need to use God's name to try to prove that what you said was true also starts in the heart – with dishonesty and deceit.

And the desire to hurt someone back who hurt you first also starts in the heart – with the need to have your own way and not give in.

Then, to those who thought that God's kingdom was about beating their enemies, Jesus offered the most surprising picture of all.

"Love your enemies," Jesus said. "Pray for those who hurt you. For God makes the sun rise on everyone – both the evil and the good!"

52. MORE KINGDOM PICTURES
Matthew 6 v 1 – 7 v 27

Next Jesus drew word pictures of proud religious people.

"When you help the poor," Jesus said, "don't blow a trumpet so that people will see you and say how great you are. Do it in secret so that nobody knows. For God sees what you do in secret, and your reward will come from him.

"And when you pray, don't do it on the street corner to impress people. Go into your room and shut the door. Again, God sees what you do in that secret place, and your reward will come from him.
"And don't use lots of fancy words when you pray. God already knows what you need."

Then Jesus gave an example of a plain and honest kind of prayer...

"Our Father in heaven, your name is holy.
Please make your kingdom grow.
Please make your plans happen on earth,
just as they do in heaven.
Please give us the food we need to live today.
Forgive the wrong things we have done,
as we forgive those who hurt us.
Help us not to be tempted to do what's wrong.
And save us from all evil."

Jesus painted a picture of treasure next. Treasure stolen. Treasure turned to dust and rust.
"Don't spend your life looking for that kind of treasure," he said, "for it does not last. Save up treasure in heaven instead.
"You have to choose what you give your life to. To God? Or to things? You can't serve both!"

Then there were pictures of birds and flowers.

"God feeds those birds," Jesus said. "God dresses those lilies more beautifully than Solomon in his finest clothes. So don't worry about what you will eat or wear. Worry is for people who don't believe in God.

"He knows what you need. So trust him. Make living his kingdom life the most important thing. And he will take care of the rest!"

Next Jesus drew a picture of one person with a tiny speck in their eye and another person with a log sticking out of theirs!

"Don't judge," he said. "Take the log out of your own eye before you start looking for specks in someone else's eye."

Then there was a picture of a door, of bread and stones, and of a fish and a snake.

"Knock on God's door for what you need," Jesus said. "And the door will open. Remember that he's your Father and that he loves you. So he won't give you a stone if you ask for bread, or a snake if you ask for a fish.

"Treat other people the way you want them to treat you," Jesus said. "That's the Law and the Prophets wrapped up in one!"

Finally, Jesus told a story about two houses.

"A wise man built his house on a rock. And when the rain fell and the wind blew and the waters rose, the man's house stood firm.

"A foolish man built his house on sand. And when the rain fell and the wind blew and the waters rose, that man's house fell down with a crash.

"Who is the wise man who built his house on a rock?" Jesus asked. "Everyone who hears the words I have to say and puts them into action!"

53. THE KING ON THE DONKEY
MATTHEW 21 v 1-11; LUKE 19 v 28-40

Jesus taught about the kingdom of God. He told parables about the kingdom of God. He performed miracles to show that God's kingdom was near. He healed people and stopped storms and fed thousands with a bit of fish and bread. But when he came to Bethany, outside of Jerusalem, he did something that grabbed the attention of everyone who lived near the city.

He raised his friend Lazarus from the dead!

So everyone was buzzing in the run-up to the Passover feast, when Jesus reached the top of the hill that led down into Jerusalem.

"If you go into the nearby village," Jesus told two of his disciples, "you will find a young donkey that has never been ridden. Untie it and bring it to me. And if anyone asks what you're doing, tell them that I need it."

The disciples did as Jesus asked. And when they returned with the young donkey, they put their cloaks on its back, and Jesus hopped on for a ride.

But this wasn't just any ride – it wasn't just a slightly unusual way of making the trip down the hill. No, Jesus did all of this on purpose. For he remembered an old prophecy – from the words of Zechariah – which said that Israel's promised King, their Messiah, would come to them humbly, riding on a donkey. Not as a conqueror but as a meek and loving servant. And he hoped the crowds would remember it too.

After the excitement of Jesus raising Lazarus from the dead, the crowds remembered well! And they jumped at the chance to celebrate Jesus as the King for whom they had waited for so long.

Some laid cloaks on the road before him. Others cut branches from palm trees and spread them along the route.

And everyone shouted, "Save us, Son of David! Hosanna in the highest! Blessed is the King, who comes in God's name!"

Well, not everyone actually. The religious leaders did not join in the celebration. Instead, they muttered among themselves, saying, "Look, the whole world is following him now!"

But when they turned to Jesus and insisted that he should tell the crowd to be quiet, his reply was plain.

"Silence them?" he said. "If I silenced these people, the stones along the road would cry out in their place!"

Rocks and stones crying out to say that Jesus was the King? Yes, that's exactly what would have happened!

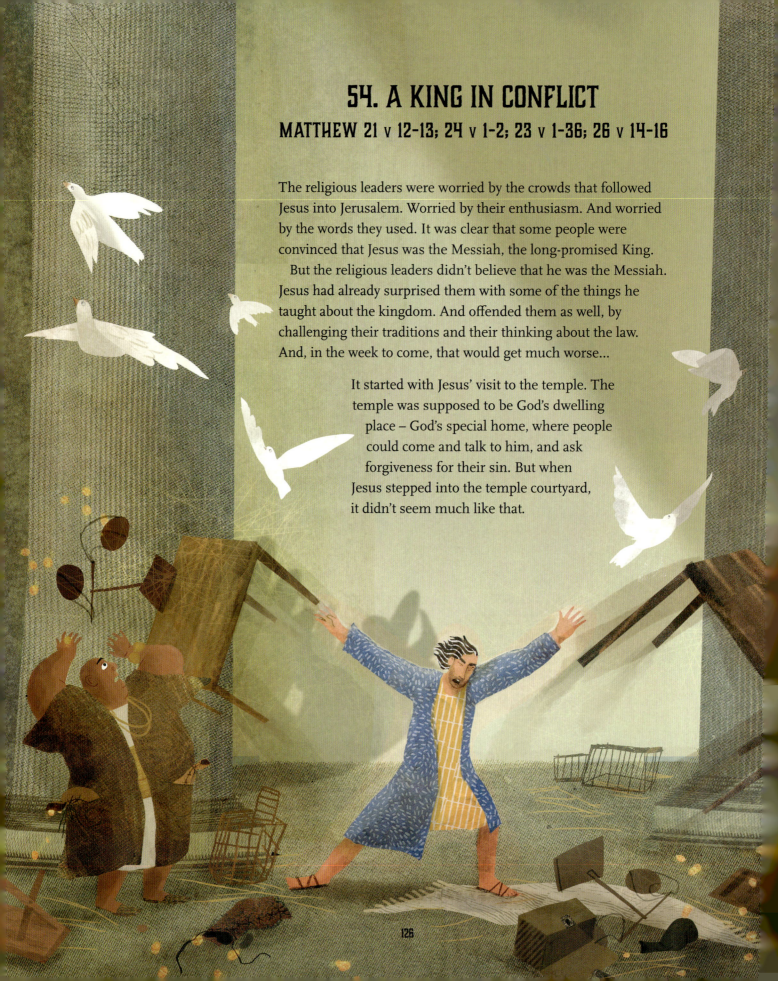

54. A KING IN CONFLICT
MATTHEW 21 v 12-13; 24 v 1-2; 23 v 1-36; 26 v 14-16

The religious leaders were worried by the crowds that followed Jesus into Jerusalem. Worried by their enthusiasm. And worried by the words they used. It was clear that some people were convinced that Jesus was the Messiah, the long-promised King.

But the religious leaders didn't believe that he was the Messiah. Jesus had already surprised them with some of the things he taught about the kingdom. And offended them as well, by challenging their traditions and their thinking about the law. And, in the week to come, that would get much worse...

It started with Jesus' visit to the temple. The temple was supposed to be God's dwelling place – God's special home, where people could come and talk to him, and ask forgiveness for their sin. But when Jesus stepped into the temple courtyard, it didn't seem much like that.

People could only spend the special temple coins when they were there, so they had to change their ordinary money for those coins. Sadly, the money-changers took advantage of this and charged far more than they should.

The same was true of the people who sold the sacrificial birds. Jesus' parents had sacrificed a couple of doves when he was born – remember? But if people couldn't bring their own birds with them, they had to buy them at the temple. And, sadly, the bird-sellers took advantage of that, just like the money-changers.

The temple was supposed to be God's special home, where people could come and talk to him. But other people were making money out of this and cheating those who had come to talk to God!

Understandably, this made Jesus angry. So, in an act that looked very much like what the prophets did, Jesus turned over the tables of the money-changers. And the seats of the dove-sellers as well. He even used the words of the prophets Isaiah and Jeremiah as he did it.

"My house should be a place for prayer!" Jesus said. "But you have turned it into a hideout for robbers!"

The religious leaders who oversaw what happened at the temple were not at all pleased. How dare Jesus speak like that about THEIR temple?

But it got worse.

Much like the prophet Jeremiah, Jesus also spoke of a time in the future when the temple would be destroyed.

"Not one stone will stand upon another," he predicted.

(And, sure enough, around 40 years later, that is exactly what happened.)

Jesus knew that God had a plan for an even better temple. Instead of dwelling in a building made of stones, God would make his special home in *people*—in Jesus' followers! There would be no more money-changing or bird-buying then. Talking to God would be as easy as talking to the person next to you—or even easier. And this would all happen because of Jesus.

But the religious leaders didn't like Jesus, and they were horrified by the idea that THEIR temple would be destroyed.

It didn't help that Jesus spent much of that week criticising those leaders with another set of his famous prophetic pictures.

"They are like blind guides," Jesus said, "who don't know the way to God and lead others astray with them.

"They are like cups," Jesus said. "Clean on the outside but dirty with greed and selfishness inside.

"They are like white-washed tombs," he went on. "Hypocrites who look shiny and good but are filled with dead men's bones!"

The religious leaders had heard enough. Jesus had to go!

So they offered Judas Iscariot, one of Jesus' disciples, 30 pieces of silver to betray him...

55. THE KING'S SUPPER
LUKE 22 v 7-23, 39-46

It was Passover time. That's why Jesus was in Jerusalem. To be just like those first Passover lambs, whose blood was smeared on the doorposts and lintels to set God's people free from slavery in Egypt – remember? For the time had come for Jesus to shed his blood, too, to set everyone free from the slavery of sin and death. To be the child who crushed the serpent's head. To be the Messiah King, whose wounds would heal the world.

So when Peter and John asked him where he wanted to eat the Passover meal, he gave them these instructions...

"Go into the city. You will be met by a man carrying a water jar. Follow him to his master's house. And when you get there, say to the master, 'Where is the guest room where our teacher can celebrate the Passover with his disciples?'

"He will take you to a large, furnished upstairs room. Prepare the Passover meal there."

So that's what the disciples did. They found the water-jar man. They followed him to his master's house. They were shown to the upstairs room. And there they prepared the Passover meal.

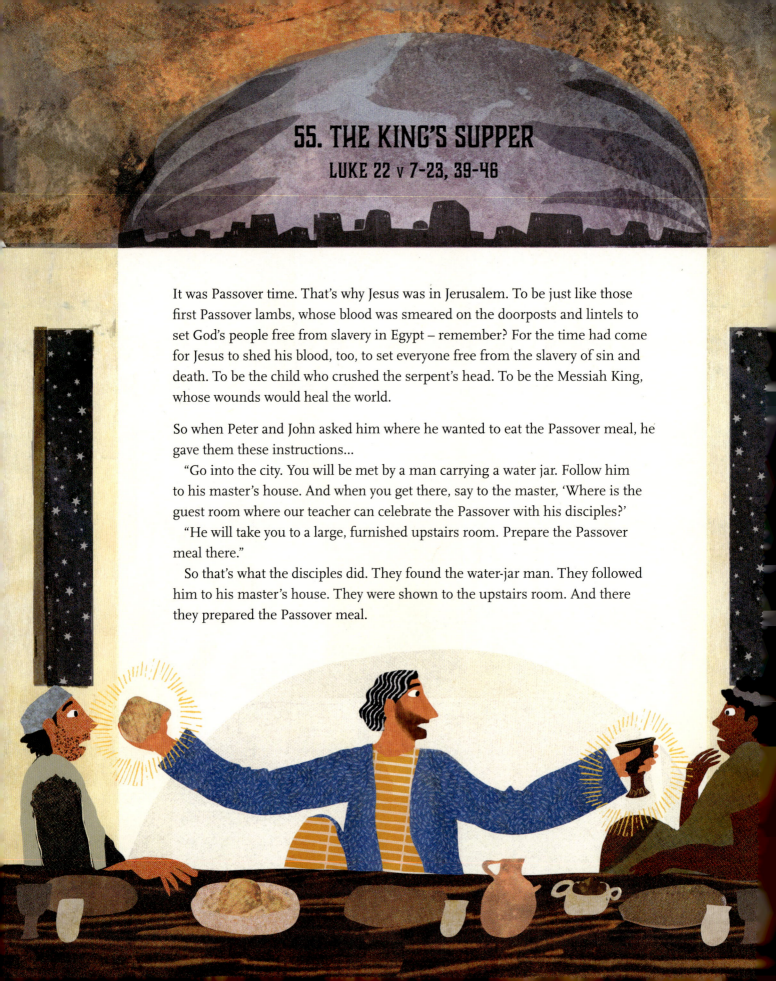

While they were eating, Jesus said to his disciples, "I very much wanted to eat this Passover meal with you before I suffered. For I will not eat it again until all that this meal stands for comes true in my Father's kingdom."

Then Jesus took a cup of wine, gave thanks for it and told his disciples to share it among themselves.

"I won't drink wine again either," he said, "until God's kingdom comes".

Then he took bread and gave thanks for that too. He broke it and gave it to his disciples, saying, "This is my body. I give it for you. Do this to remember me."

And when they had eaten the bread, he took the cup of wine and said, "This wine poured out for you is my blood – which brings about God's new kingly covenant promise".

When he had finished, Jesus turned to them all and said sadly, "The person who will betray me is here, at this table. What will to happen to me has to happen. But woe to the one who brings it about."

And, at once, the disciples questioned one another, trying to figure out which one of them it was.

When the meal was over, they went to the Mount of Olives. Jesus told his disciples to stay and pray, while he walked away – about a stone's throw.

Then, falling to his knees, Jesus prayed, "Father, if you will, please, take this cup – this thing I must do – away from me. But if it's what you really want, then I will do it!"

An angel came to give him strength, but Jesus was still so upset about what the coming day would bring that his sweat dropped like blood to the ground.

And when his prayers were finished and he went back to his disciples, he found them all asleep.

All but one, that is – Judas the betrayer, who had gone to tell Jesus' enemies exactly where he was...

56. THE KING ON TRIAL

JOHN 18 v 1 – 19 v 16

Judas knew all about the garden where Jesus had taken his disciples to pray. He'd been there many times, himself. So that's where he led the high priest's soldiers. They had torches and lanterns and swords.

Jesus knew what they wanted, but he bravely stepped forward and asked them anyway, "Who are you looking for?"

"Jesus of Nazareth," they replied.

And when Jesus said, "I am he," they took a step backwards and then fell to the ground.

So he asked them again who they wanted. And then Jesus simply said, "I already told you. I am Jesus. Now, let these other men go."

But Peter had different plans. If Jesus wouldn't defend himself, then Peter would. So he drew his sword and waved it about, but only managed to cut off the ear of one of the high priest's servants.

"Put your sword away," Jesus told him. "I have to go with them. It's what my Father wants."

So the soldiers tied up Jesus and took him to Annas, the high priest's father-in-law. Annas asked Jesus all kinds of questions about the things he taught.

"Why are you asking me this?" Jesus replied. "I have spoken openly in the temple and synagogues. I have no secrets. If you want to know what I teach, ask the people who heard me."

At that, one of the officers punched Jesus.

"That's no way to answer!" he shouted.

"If what I've said is wrong," Jesus replied, "then show me. But don't hit me if I'm right!"

And with that, they dragged Jesus to Caiaphas, the high priest, and from there to Pilate, the Roman governor.

It was morning by this time, and Pilate came out to meet them.

"So, what is this man accused of?" Pilate asked.

"We wouldn't have brought him to you if he hadn't done anything wrong," they replied.

"Then judge him by your own laws," said Pilate.

"He needs to be put to death," they answered. "And your laws say we don't have the right to do that."

So Pilate took Jesus inside and asked him plainly, "Are you the king of the Jews?"

"I am a king," Jesus answered. "But not the kind of king you're thinking of. If I was that kind of king, my followers would be fighting for me. But my kingdom is not from this world."

So Pilate went back to the chief priests and said, "This man is guilty of nothing! But seeing as I can release a prisoner at Passover time, how about I let this Jesus go?"

"No!" they shouted. "Release Barabbas instead!" Jesus had done nothing wrong. But Barabbas was a thief and a murderer.

Then Pilate had Jesus whipped. His soldiers jammed a crown made of thorns on Jesus' head. They put a purple robe on his shoulders and beat and mocked him.

But if Pilate thought that would be enough to satisfy the chief priests, he was wrong.

"Crucify him! Crucify him!" they cried. "If you let him go, you are no friend of Caesar."

And, with the saddest words of all, the very people to whom God had sent his long-promised King shouted out their loyalty to the earthly king who had conquered and ill-treated them.

"We have no king but Caesar!"

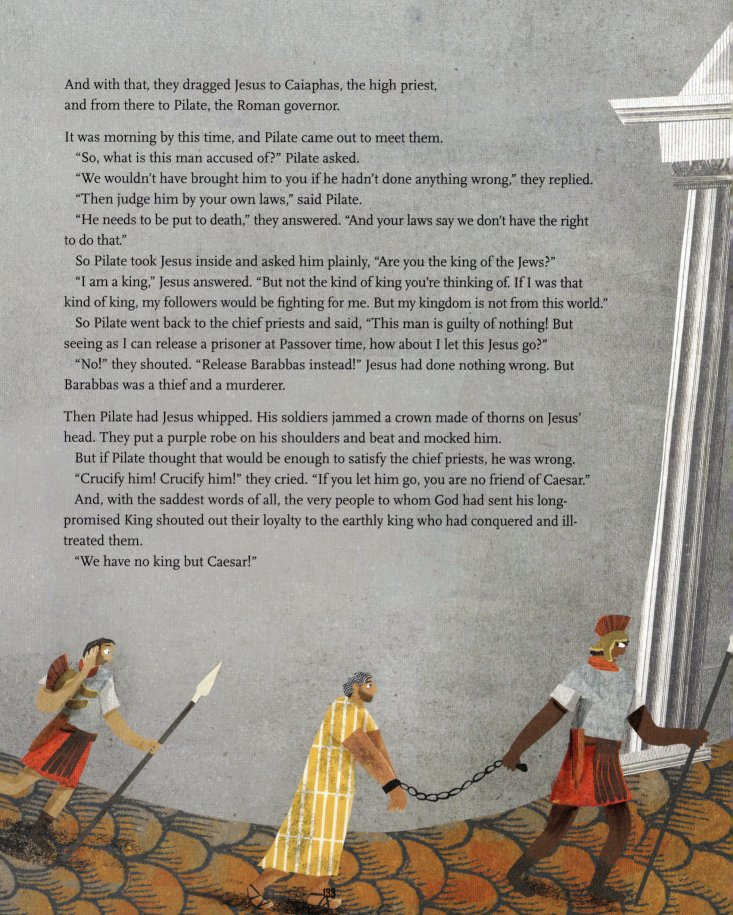

57. THE KING IS DEAD
MARK 15 v 16-47

Having beaten Jesus and mocked him and jammed a crown of thorns on his head, the Roman soldiers led him out of the palace. Along the way, they forced a man called Simon to carry Jesus' cross.

Out of the city they went and up to a killing hill called, "The Place of the Skull".

To help Jesus deal with the pain, the soldiers offered him wine mixed with myrrh (one of the gifts of the star-watchers, all those years ago – remember?). But Jesus wouldn't drink it.

Then they nailed his hands and feet to the cross, propped it up between two others, and stuck a sign at the top of the cross that read, "The King of the Jews".

The sign was meant as a cruel joke, but as the soldiers divided up Jesus' clothes and gambled for them, they had no idea how right those words actually were.

The people passing by were no less cruel.

"You said you'd destroy our temple and build it again in three days!" they mocked. "Well, if you can do that, you can surely come down off that cross!"

They completely misunderstood what Jesus meant, of course – that *he* was God's temple, the place where God would now dwell with his people. And as for the three days, well...

But there was more mocking to come.

"He saved other people," laughed the chief priests, "so why can't he save himself? And if he really is the Messiah and our long-promised King, let him come down from the cross and prove it!"

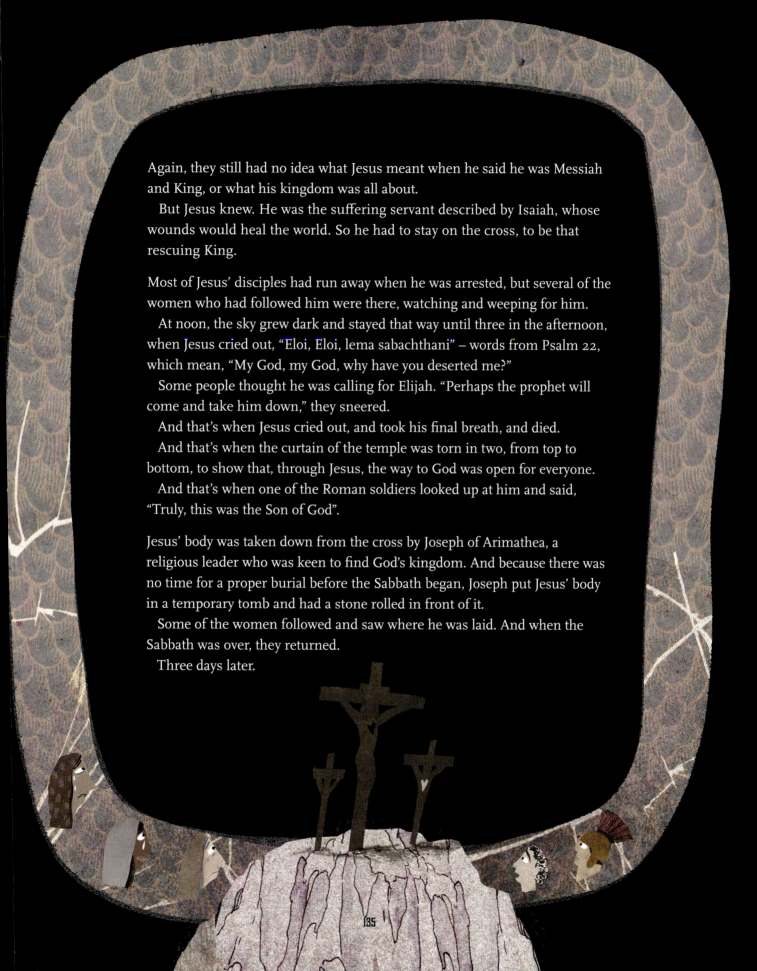

Again, they still had no idea what Jesus meant when he said he was Messiah and King, or what his kingdom was all about.

But Jesus knew. He was the suffering servant described by Isaiah, whose wounds would heal the world. So he had to stay on the cross, to be that rescuing King.

Most of Jesus' disciples had run away when he was arrested, but several of the women who had followed him were there, watching and weeping for him.

At noon, the sky grew dark and stayed that way until three in the afternoon, when Jesus cried out, "Eloi, Eloi, lema sabachthani" – words from Psalm 22, which mean, "My God, my God, why have you deserted me?"

Some people thought he was calling for Elijah. "Perhaps the prophet will come and take him down," they sneered.

And that's when Jesus cried out, and took his final breath, and died.

And that's when the curtain of the temple was torn in two, from top to bottom, to show that, through Jesus, the way to God was open for everyone.

And that's when one of the Roman soldiers looked up at him and said, "Truly, this was the Son of God".

Jesus' body was taken down from the cross by Joseph of Arimathea, a religious leader who was keen to find God's kingdom. And because there was no time for a proper burial before the Sabbath began, Joseph put Jesus' body in a temporary tomb and had a stone rolled in front of it.

Some of the women followed and saw where he was laid. And when the Sabbath was over, they returned.

Three days later.

58. LONG LIVE THE KING! A MYSTERIOUS SHOCK
LUKE 24 v 1-12

On the first day of the week, when the Sabbath was over, some of the women who had followed Jesus went to the tomb to put sweet-smelling spices on his body.

Among them were Mary Magdalene and Joanna and Mary the mother of James.

When they arrived, they discovered that the stone that Joseph of Arimathea had rolled across the front of the tomb had somehow been rolled away.

It was a mystery!

So into the tomb they crept. And, more mysterious still, the body of Jesus was no longer there.

As they were scratching their heads and wondering what had happened, two men suddenly appeared beside them. But they didn't look like ordinary men. (For a start, they were shining bright and white!) The women were terrified and bowed their heads to the ground before them.

"Why are you looking in a tomb for someone who is alive?" the men asked. "Jesus isn't here. He has risen!

"Cast your minds back to when you were in Galilee with him. He told you then that the Messiah would have to be handed over to evil men. That he would need to be crucified. And that in three days he would rise from the dead."

"So he did!" said the women to each other, remembering Jesus' words and putting them all together.

So, having worked out the mystery, they ran off to tell Jesus' disciples the good news.

Sadly, the disciples were not impressed. In fact, they dismissed what the women had seen and heard as a silly story. They thought they'd made it up!

But Peter wasn't so sure. So he went to the tomb to see for himself. He crept in, just like the women. And all he found were the linen cloths in which Jesus' body had been wrapped.

Now he had a mystery to solve as well!

59. LONG LIVE THE KING! A VERY LONG WALK
LUKE 24 v 13-35

When the women who found the empty tomb went back to the followers of Jesus to tell them what they saw, there were more than just the eleven disciples in that room.

There was a man called Cleopas, for a start, who lived in a village called Emmaus, about seven miles* from Jerusalem. And there was someone who lived there with him. A friend? A lodger? Or, quite possibly, it was Mrs. Cleopas.

Anyway, following the women's report and Peter's hasty run to the tomb to check out their story, Cleopas and his companion walked back to Emmaus, discussing everything that had happened that day.

Along the way, Jesus wandered up and walked alongside them. But, somehow, he managed to make sure they did not recognise him.

"So, what are you two talking about?" he asked.

"Seriously?" Cleopas replied. "You must be the only visitor to Jerusalem that doesn't know what's happened there these past few days."

"What?" Jesus asked. "Tell me."

"The things that happened to Jesus of Nazareth!" Cleopas replied. "He was a prophet. He did mighty things. He spoke powerful words. Sadly, the chief priests and religious leaders turned him over to the Romans, who crucified him. But we had hoped he was the Messiah – the one come to save our people.

"Here's the thing, though. It's been three days since he died. And, this morning, some of the women in our group went to his tomb and could not find his body. Instead, they saw angels, who told them that Jesus was alive! Others went to check, and they couldn't find his body either!"

"Oh, foolish ones," Jesus replied. "Why are you so slow to believe what the prophets have already told us? It was always the case that the Messiah would need to suffer before entering into the glory that God prepared for him."

*about 11 km

Then, starting with Moses and the Prophets, he showed them everything that the Old Testament Scriptures had to say about him.

(Things that we remember, right? That we saw in Isaiah and the other prophets. That his wounds would heal the world but God would not leave him in his grave.)

As they approached Emmaus, Jesus acted as if he was going further, but Cleopas and his companion kindly said, "It's getting late. Why don't you stay with us?"

Jesus agreed, and while they were eating, he broke the bread and gave thanks for it. And that's when they knew. It wasn't some stranger they'd been passing the time with. It was Jesus!

With that, he vanished, and they were left amazed.

"Didn't our hearts grow warm inside us as he taught us from the Scriptures?" they said to each other.

And that very same hour, they hurried those seven miles back to Jerusalem!

And when they found the others, everyone had a story to tell.

"Peter saw him! He's alive!" said those who had stayed in Jerusalem.

"And we saw him too!" said Cleopas and his companion. "The moment he broke the bread!"

60. LONG LIVE THE KING!
THE DOOR WAS LOCKED
LUKE 24 v 36-49

Cleopas and his companion had just walked seven miles back to Jerusalem.

"We saw Jesus!" they told the disciples.

"Peter saw him too!" the disciples replied.

And at that very moment, even though the door was locked, Jesus appeared.

And everybody saw him!

"Peace be with you," he said, as if it was an ordinary greeting on some ordinary day.

But there was nothing ordinary about it, as far as the disciples were concerned. They were startled. And frightened. And thought he was a ghost.

"Why are you troubled?" Jesus asked. "And why do you doubt? Look at my hands. Look at my feet. It's me! It really is!

"Touch me, if you like. You'll see.

"Ghosts don't have bones. Ghosts don't have skin. But I do!"

Jesus showed them his hands and his feet. And they still didn't know what to think. It was almost too good to be true!

So Jesus asked if they had anything to eat. They gave him a piece of fish. He gobbled it up. That's not the kind of thing a ghost could do.

Then he had a word with them. Well, quite a lot of words actually!

"When I was with you, I told you that everything the Old Testament Scriptures said about me – in the Law of Moses, in the Prophets and in the Psalms – had to happen."

Then he went through those Scriptures again to help them understand what he meant by that.

"The words are there! The Messiah had to suffer. He was always meant to rise from the dead on the third day. And now the need for repentance from sin and the opportunity for forgiveness needs to be told to everyone in every country, starting with Jerusalem."

(And we remember that, don't we? Because we read those Scriptures too. The Messiah was never meant to be a conquering King. No, he was always supposed to be the servant King, who died to take away our sin and rose to pave our way to life for ever, and was sent, not only for the children of Abraham but to make real God's promise to Abraham, and to bless the whole world.)

"You are my witnesses," Jesus told them. "You have watched me and listened to me and seen me alive again! So you are the ones who need to tell everyone what you saw.

"You'll need God's power to help you do that though. So stay in Jerusalem until my Father gives you the gift that he has promised!"

61. THE KING ASCENDS
LUKE 24 v 50-53; ACTS 1 v 6-11

Forty days. That's how long the risen Jesus stayed with his followers and his friends in his new resurrected body. A body that could appear suddenly out of nowhere, but could also eat and be touched and be recognised.

He met with some of his friends on a beach. He met with some on their own. And, on one occasion, he met with 500 people at once!

When it was time for him to go, Jesus led his disciples to Bethany.

"When will you give back the kingdom to Israel?" they asked.

"The timing of such things is not for you to know," Jesus replied. "That's my Father's business. What you do need to know is that you will receive power when the Holy Spirit comes upon you. And you will tell people everything you have seen and heard about me – from Jerusalem to Judea, to Samaria and to every other place in the world!"

And when he had said that, Jesus ascended – which means he was lifted up, right in front of them all, and disappeared into a cloud!

They stood there, open-mouthed, staring into the sky.

And that is when two men in white robes appeared to them and said…

"Men of Galilee, why are you standing around looking up into the sky? Jesus was taken up to heaven. And from heaven he will one day return."

And, in response, the disciples worshipped Jesus.

They went back to Jerusalem, joyfully, to wait for the promised Holy Spirit.

And they went to the temple as well, daily, to give thanks to God.

And what about Jesus? Where did he go?

He ascended to heaven.
He ascended, the victor over death and sin.
He ascended, the one who had crushed the serpent's head.
He ascended, to speak to God on our behalf.
He ascended, to rule over everyone and everything, at his Father's side.
He ascended to be King!

62. THE HOLY SPIRIT COMES
ACTS 2 v 1-41

Waiting. That's what Jesus' disciples were doing.

Waiting in Jerusalem, just as he'd told them.

Waiting for the gift he had promised to send them.

It was the Feast of Pentecost, a time of thanksgiving for the firstfruits of the harvest and a celebration of the law that God gave to Moses. So Jews from all around the world were gathered in Jerusalem.

And that is when the Holy Spirit came. The firstfruit of all the new things that God would give his people through Jesus. And the presence of God himself within them, writing his law on their hearts!

The Spirit came with the sound of a rushing wind. A sound that filled the house where they were waiting.

The Spirit came with fire too. (Just as John the Baptist said would happen – remember?) And tongues of fire sat, flashing and flickering, upon each head.

Then there were other tongues – the languages of all the different people waiting outside. The means to spread the story of Jesus to the world!

At the sound of the wind and of the words (a bit like Creation, remember?), the crowds gathered and wondered.

"We're from every part of the world," they said. "And these are just uneducated people from Galilee. How is it that they are speaking to us in our native languages?"

"They're not speaking! They're babbling!" someone shouted, from the back. "They're drunk!"

And that's when Peter stood up to explain to the crowd exactly what was happening.

First, he told them that nobody was drunk.

"It's only nine o'clock in the morning!" he said.

Next, he reminded them that God had promised this would happen, by the words of his prophet Joel.

"In the last days, God says, 'I will pour out my Spirit on everyone! They will all speak like prophets, and everyone who calls on my name will be saved.'"

Then Peter told them how this had happened.

"It's all down to Jesus. You saw his mighty works, and yet you crucified him. But God raised him from the dead.

"King David saw this, years ago. In a psalm, he said that God would not let his holy one stay in the place of the dead and rot away.

"David wasn't talking about himself. We all know where his tomb is! But God did promise David that one of his descendants would reign on his throne for ever. And that's who David was talking about...

"Jesus, who was raised by God.
Jesus, whose resurrection we witnessed.
Jesus, who now rules at God's right hand.
Jesus, who sent the Holy Spirit and everything you see today.
Jesus, whom God made Messiah and King.
Jesus, whom you put to death on a cross!"

When they heard this and realised what they had done, the people were heartbroken. "What should we do about this?" they cried.

"Repent of what you have done," said Peter. "Be baptised in Jesus' name for the forgiveness of your sins. And you too will receive the gift of his Holy Spirit."

So that's what they did. Three thousand of them.

The firstfruits of God's new harvest!

63. BRINGING THE KINGDOM TO LIFE
ACTS 2 v 42-47

Three thousand people became followers of Jesus on the day of Pentecost. And, right away, they worked together to bring to life what Jesus had taught about the kingdom of God.

For a start, they were very keen to find out everything they could about Jesus the Messiah and King.

"Tell us what he said!" they asked. "Tell us what he did! Did he really bring Lazarus back from the dead? Did he really walk on water?"

And the apostles were more than happy to tell them. They were the eleven disciples who had been with Jesus from the start, plus a man called Matthias, who was chosen to replace Judas. They were the ones Jesus had chosen to be his witnesses to the world, helped by the power of the Holy Spirit.

So, day by day, the apostles thrilled the followers of Jesus with all they remembered about what he had said and done.

But it wasn't enough for them simply to know about Jesus' life and what he had taught about the kingdom. They had to learn how to put what he taught into practice as well – to live it themselves.

So they hung out together. They ate meals together. They learned to love and accept and forgive each other, just as Jesus loved and accepted and forgave the people he met.

They ate one special meal in particular – the supper that Jesus had shared with his disciples before he died. They broke the bread and drank the wine to remember all that Jesus the Messiah and King had done for them.

And they prayed!

Jesus had shown his disciples how to pray. Remember the prayer he taught them? And that's because Jesus knew that praying was the way to stay close to God and was the key to living life in God's kingdom. So the followers of Jesus prayed together, to get closer and closer to God, and to grow in their trust in him.

And then there were miracles. Of course there were!

Following Jesus' example and helped by his Spirit, the apostles performed healing miracles, just as their Messiah and King had done.

Every day, Jesus' followers went to the temple to thank God and to worship him. For they knew that worshipping God was the way to say thank you for all those miracles, and yet another way of staying close to him.

And when they got close to God, they knew that he was the one they needed to put their trust in – and not in the things they owned. (Jesus taught that, remember?)

So they happily gave away their possessions to help those who didn't have what they needed. In fact, they acted as if nothing belonged to them and chose to sell what they had to help others.

And what happened?

People liked what they were doing and were keen to join them. And their numbers kept growing and growing!

64. THE BEAUTIFUL GATE

ACTS 3 v 1 – 4 v 22

It was three o'clock in the afternoon, and Peter and John were on their way to the temple, to pray.

Outside the gate called Beautiful, they came across a man who couldn't walk. Not from the time when he was born.

The man begged them for some money. It's what he did every day.

"Look at us," said Peter and John. And the man did, expecting to be given a coin or two. But he got something else instead.

"I don't have any silver," said Peter, "or any gold either. But I'll give you what I *do* have. In the name of Jesus of Nazareth, the Messiah, stand up and walk."

Then Peter took him by the hand and lifted him to his feet. And, sure enough, his ankles and feet grew strong. And he not only walked; he went into the temple, praising God and leaping for joy!

A crowd gathered, amazed. So Peter stood up in Solomon's Porch and explained what had happened.

"Why are you staring at us?" he asked. "This didn't happen because we are good or powerful. No, Jesus did this!

"You handed him over to Pilate to be executed. And even when Pilate found him innocent and gave you a choice, you decided to free a murderer instead.

"That's right, you killed the Author of life. But the God of Abraham and Isaac and Jacob raised Jesus from the dead and glorified him. And we are witnesses to that.

"Granted, you had no idea of what you were doing. Neither did your leaders. And, yes, God said, through his prophets, that the Messiah would need to suffer. And that is what happened.

"But the time has come to change your mind about Jesus, to say sorry for what you have done, and to ask for God's forgiveness.

"Even Moses said that God would send a prophet like him to his people. The prophets repeated that down the ages. And you are the children of Abraham, with whom God made a kingly covenant promise – that the world would be blessed through his family. So let God bless you now and turn away from the wicked thing you have done."

And 2,000 people in that crowd believed what Peter said and became followers of Jesus.

But when the religious leaders heard that Peter and John were telling the people about Jesus' resurrection, they were not pleased. And they arrested them.

The next day, Peter and John were brought before the high priest and the other religious leaders to be questioned.

"By what power and in whose name did you do this?" they asked.

And Peter answered.

"If we're being questioned about doing a good deed for a man who couldn't walk, then know this. He was healed by the power of Jesus, God's Messiah, whom you rejected and killed. It is only by his name that we can be saved."

What could the leaders do? Everyone had seen the healing. The crowd was on Peter and John's side. So they told them to stop talking about Jesus.

And Peter's reply was clear and to the point,

"We're going to do what God tells us. Not men!"

65. SAUL SEES THE KING
ACTS 7 v 54 – 8 v 3; 9 v 1-19

More and more people became followers of Jesus. They believed that Jesus was God's long-promised Messiah and King. But there were plenty of other people who disagreed. Strongly.

In fact, when one of Jesus' followers – a man called Stephen – told the story of Abraham's family, with Jesus as the answer to all the promises, some people were so angry that they dragged him outside the city walls and stoned him to death.

Watching their coats – as it was hard work throwing heavy stones – was a young man called Saul. He was a Pharisee, trained in the Jewish law by a rabbi called Gamaliel. And he was so sure that the followers of Jesus were wrong about Jesus' resurrection and his claim to be Messiah that Saul made it his personal mission to arrest them and throw them into prison.

In the face of threats like that, many of the followers of Jesus left Jerusalem and fled to other parts of Judea and to Samaria.

Some even went as far as Damascus, in Syria.

So Saul went to the high priest and asked for permission to go to Damascus in the hope of finding the followers of Jesus and arresting them.

But on the way to Damascus, Saul found something else. The very last thing he expected.

A bright light shone down from heaven and surrounded him.

He fell to the ground. And that's when he heard a voice.

"Saul! Saul! Why do you persecute me?"

Trembling, Saul replied, "Who are you, Lord?"

And the answer made him tremble even more.

"I am Jesus. It's me you're persecuting. So get up. Go into Damascus. And you will be told what to do."

Tyras
Chersonesus
Panticapaeum
R. B O S
Sindi
Cercetae
Taurica
Theudosia
Bosp. Cimmerius
Phanagoria
Troesmis
Chersonesus
Heraclea
Ister F.
Durostorum
Prista
PONTUS EUXINUS
Odessus
Marcianop.
Haemus M.
Sinope
Philipp.
Apollonia
Amastris
Paphlag
THRACIA
Adrianopolis
Heraclea
Halys F.
Rhodope M.
Byzantium
Nicomedia
Gangra
Amasia
Propont.
Nicaea
BITHYNIA
Ancyra
Prusa
GALATIA
Tavium
Sebastia
Cyz.
Mysia
Alex Troas
Pergamum
Dorylaeum
Pessinus
Caesarea
Melitene
Mare
ASIA
CAPPADOCIA
Lesbos
Magn.
Sardes
Antioch.
Chios
Smyrna
Athenae
Samos
Ephesus
Laodicea
Apamea
Icon.
Cyclades
Miletus
Caria
Pisidia
PAMPHYL.
Isauria
Adana
Hierap.
Halicarnassus
LYC.
Attalia
Seleucia
Tarsus
Beroea
Aegaeum
Rhodus
Xanthus
ANTIOCHIA
Apam.
Salamis
Cnosus
Paphos
CYPRUS
Aradus
CRETA
Berytus
Tyrus
Ptolemais
Caesarea

When Saul stood up, he could not see. So the men with him led him into the city. And there he waited for three days, without eating or drinking a thing.

In the meantime, Jesus appeared to one of his followers who lived in Damascus. A man called Ananias.

"Go to Straight Street," Jesus told him, "to the house of Judas. Saul from Tarsus is staying there. I have given him a vision – a picture of you laying hands on him so his sight will be returned."

And now it was Ananias' turn to tremble.

"Saul of Tarsus!" he cried. "Everyone knows about the evil things he has done to your followers in Jerusalem. And now he has come here, to do the same to us!"

"I have chosen him," Jesus replied, "to tell my story to our people, and to the Gentiles, and even to kings! So, go!"

Off Ananias went. And when he found Saul, he laid his hands on him so he would be filled with the Holy Spirit and see again.

Something that seemed like fish scales fell from Saul's eyes. And he could see again. He could see the things in front of him, and he could also see that Jesus was everything his followers said he was!

So Saul was baptised. And he ate. And when he was strong enough, he went out into Damascus to tell everyone that Jesus was, indeed, Messiah and King!

66. AN ETHIOPIAN FOLLOWS THE KING
ACTS 8 v 4-8, 26-39

When the followers of Jesus fled from Jerusalem, following the death of Stephen, some of them went to Samaria. Jesus had told them that they would need to tell the people of Samaria about him, so this was the perfect opportunity.

And Philip was the perfect man for the job!

Like Stephen, he had been chosen by the apostles to organise the feeding of poor widows who didn't have enough to eat. And, like Stephen, he was wise and good, and was filled with God's Holy Spirit.

So when he told the people of Samaria about Jesus, they listened to him. And when he cast out evil spirits and healed people who could not walk, they were filled with joy and wanted to follow Jesus too!

But Jesus wasn't satisfied with his story spreading just to Samaria. No, the whole world needed to hear about him.

So an angel appeared to Philip and sent him somewhere else.

"Go to the road that runs from Jerusalem to Gaza," the angel said.

Now that road was out in the wilderness, more or less in the middle of nowhere. A strange place to send someone who was used to telling crowds about Jesus.

But Philip did what the angel told him to do. And, sure enough, it wasn't long before a chariot came rolling by. Not one of those fast racing chariots you might have seen in gladiator films, but something more like a horse-drawn coach, with a driver and a passenger. A very important passenger, as it happens – the chief treasurer of the queen of Ethiopia!

He had been to Jerusalem to worship God. And as he went, he was reading out loud from the prophet Isaiah.

"Go! Join the chariot!" the Holy Spirit told Philip.

So Philip ran up to the chariot. He heard the Ethiopian. And he asked him, "Do you understand what you're reading?"

"I could do with someone to explain it," the Ethiopian answered. And he invited Philip to sit in the chariot with him.

As it happens, it was that passage from Isaiah that we have seen before. The passage about a sheep being slaughtered and sacrificed for everyone.

"Who is the prophet talking about in this passage?" the Ethiopian asked. "Himself? Or someone else?"

Philip knew. So he told the Ethiopian all about Jesus – the good news of his life and death and resurrection. How he was God's long-promised Messiah and King. And how the Ethiopian could follow Jesus and receive his Spirit too.

And when Philip had finished, the Ethiopian spied a spot where there was some water.

"Look! Water!" he said. "What's to keep me from being baptised, right here and now?"

There wasn't anything! So the Ethiopian ordered the chariot driver to stop. He and Philip went down into the water. And Philip baptised him.

And as soon as they came up from the water, the Holy Spirit whisked Philip away!

And the Ethiopian carried on, back to his home.

The story of Jesus was spreading further and further still!

67. CORNELIUS, THE ROMAN CENTURION
ACTS 10 v 1-48

God had told Abraham that his family would be a blessing to the world.
God had told Isaiah that the Messiah would be a light to the nations.
God had told Saul that he should tell the story of Jesus to the Gentiles – people who were not Jews.
Now the time had come to make that absolutely clear.

Cornelius was a Gentile. A Roman. And a centurion in the Roman army, stationed in Caesarea. But he did not believe in the Roman gods.
No, he and his household worshipped the God of Abraham, Isaac and Jacob. He gave money to the poor. And he prayed every day.
One day, as he prayed, he had a vision of an angel.
"Cornelius," the angel said, "God has heard your prayers and seen your generosity. Send men to the home of Simon the tanner, in Joppa. Peter is staying there. Have them bring him to you."

The following day, as Cornelius' men approached Joppa, Peter was praying too – up on the flat roof of the house. Peter was hungry, and as a meal was being prepared for him, he, too, had a vision.
But it wasn't an angel he saw. No, it was something like a great big bedsheet, coming down from heaven.
And on the sheet were all kinds of animals, reptiles and birds.
"Get up, Peter!" a voice called out.
"Kill! Eat!"

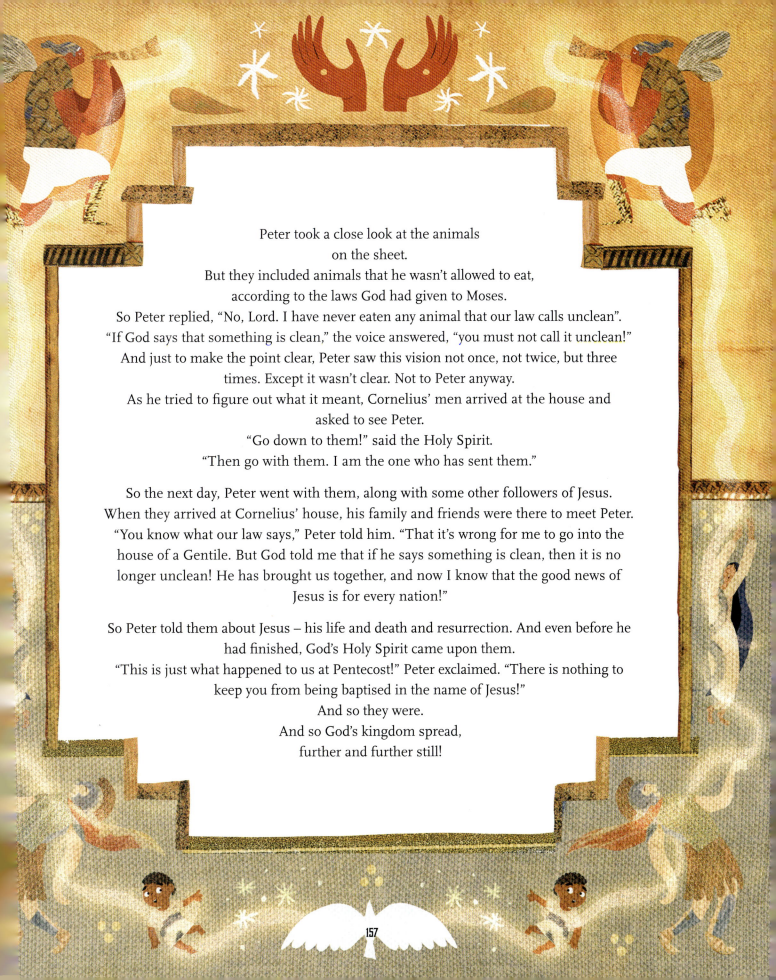

Peter took a close look at the animals
on the sheet.
But they included animals that he wasn't allowed to eat,
according to the laws God had given to Moses.
So Peter replied, "No, Lord. I have never eaten any animal that our law calls unclean".
"If God says that something is clean," the voice answered, "you must not call it unclean!"
And just to make the point clear, Peter saw this vision not once, not twice, but three
times. Except it wasn't clear. Not to Peter anyway.
As he tried to figure out what it meant, Cornelius' men arrived at the house and
asked to see Peter.
"Go down to them!" said the Holy Spirit.
"Then go with them. I am the one who has sent them."

So the next day, Peter went with them, along with some other followers of Jesus.
When they arrived at Cornelius' house, his family and friends were there to meet Peter.
"You know what our law says," Peter told him. "That it's wrong for me to go into the
house of a Gentile. But God told me that if he says something is clean, then it is no
longer unclean! He has brought us together, and now I know that the good news of
Jesus is for every nation!"

So Peter told them about Jesus – his life and death and resurrection. And even before he
had finished, God's Holy Spirit came upon them.
"This is just what happened to us at Pentecost!" Peter exclaimed. "There is nothing to
keep you from being baptised in the name of Jesus!"
And so they were.
And so God's kingdom spread,
further and further still!

68. ALL ABOUT PAUL
ACTS 9 v 20-31; 13 v 1-52; 17 v 16-34; PHILIPPIANS 2 v 5-11

Not long after Saul saw Jesus, he started travelling far and wide, telling people about him.

In each city, he and his friends visited synagogues first – places where Jews, like themselves, went to worship.

At Antioch, Saul began his talk by retracing the history of Israel, from the Exodus right through to the reign of David.

And there he stopped, to make it clear that Jesus came from David's family line.

Then Saul went on to explain that the leaders in Jerusalem had put God's chosen one to death, but that God had always meant to raise the Messiah from the dead. Saul quoted from the Psalms to make his point.

Finally, he told them that, through Jesus, forgiveness of sin was available and a freedom that the Law of Moses could not give them.

Many people in the synagogue believed what Saul said. But when some of the leaders argued with him, Saul reminded them of what Isaiah had said about God's people being a "light to the nations". Then he went and spoke to the Gentiles as well.

During this first trip, Saul started to go by his other name, Paul.

On the second trip, the Holy Spirit led him to Europe.

In Athens, Paul was invited to speak to a group of Gentiles who knew nothing about the Jewish Scriptures. So he tailored his talk to what they did know.

"In your city," he said, "I saw an altar to 'An Unknown God'. I have come to tell you about him. He is the Creator, who made heaven and earth. He is not far from us and wants us to find him. But he is not made of gold or silver or stone, like a man-made statue. He wants us to turn away from worshipping these idols, for he has appointed a man through whom he will judge us all. A man he raised from the dead!"

When they heard the phrase "raised from the dead", some of Paul's audience made fun of him. But some wanted to find out more. And, before long, some of those people put their trust in King Jesus.

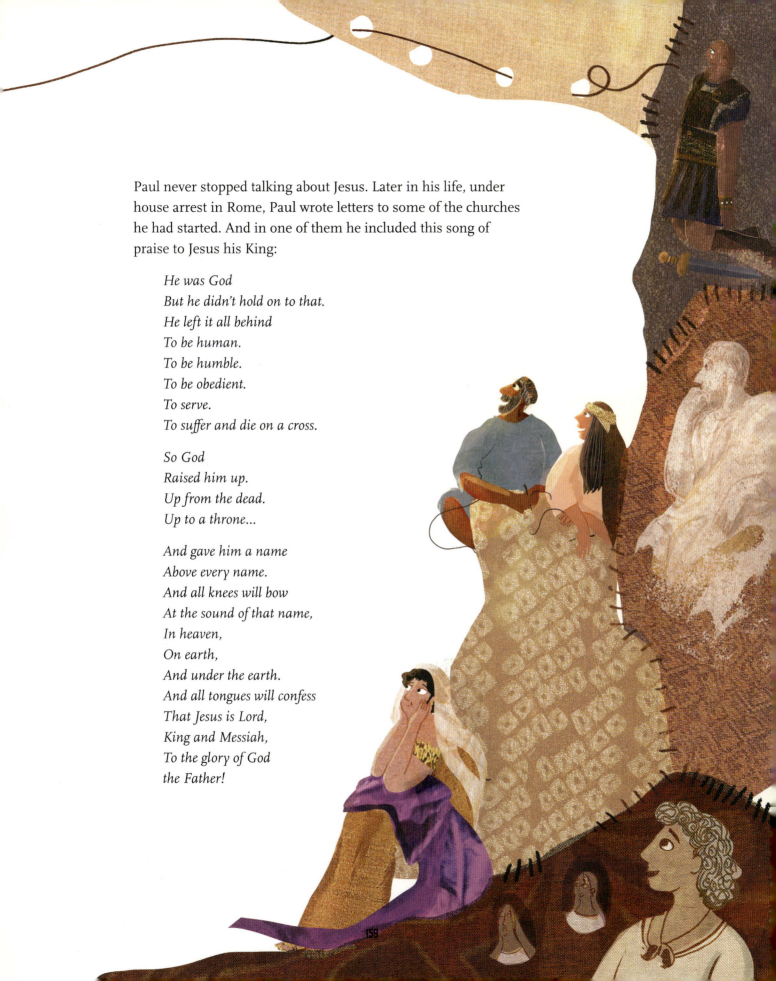

Paul never stopped talking about Jesus. Later in his life, under house arrest in Rome, Paul wrote letters to some of the churches he had started. And in one of them he included this song of praise to Jesus his King:

He was God
But he didn't hold on to that.
He left it all behind
To be human.
To be humble.
To be obedient.
To serve.
To suffer and die on a cross.

So God
Raised him up.
Up from the dead.
Up to a throne...

And gave him a name
Above every name.
And all knees will bow
At the sound of that name,
In heaven,
On earth,
And under the earth.
And all tongues will confess
That Jesus is Lord,
King and Messiah,
To the glory of God
the Father!

69. VISIONS OF THE KING
REVELATION 1 v 9-20

John lived on an island called Patmos, off the coast of Greece. But he was not there on holiday.

No, he was exiled there because the Roman emperor had decided to punish people simply because they were Christians.

While John was there, he had a vision – a strange and unusual vision designed to encourage him and all the other persecuted Christians to trust in God's power and presence, even when things were difficult.

John heard a voice first. A loud voice. A voice like a trumpet.

And the voice said, "Write a book, filled with everything you see. Then send it to the churches in Ephesus, Smyrna, Pergamum, Thyatira, Sardis, Philadelphia and Laodicea."

When John turned to see who was speaking, he saw seven golden lampstands. The speaker was there, in the midst of them.

First of all, said John, he looked like a "son of man".
(Do you remember the equally strange and unusual vision the prophet Daniel had, hundreds of years before this? He too saw a "son of man" in the vision God gave him of the coming King!)

John went on to say, "He was wearing a long robe. There was a golden sash around his chest.

"His hair was white. Like wool. Like snow.

"There was fire in his eyes. His feet shone like polished bronze. And his voice roared like rushing water.

"In his right hand he held seven stars. A sharp sword came out of his mouth. And his face was bright as the sunniest summer day."

At the sight of him, John fell frightened, like a dead man, down to the ground.

Who was this amazing and terrifying being?

Then the man in the vision laid his hand on John. And when he spoke again, John knew.

"Don't be frightened. I'm the First. I'm the Last. I'm the Living One!

"I died – and look! – I'm alive now, for ever and ever. And I have the keys to unlock death and the place of the dead."

It was Jesus! Of course it was!

Jesus the Messiah. Jesus the King.

"So, write!" said Jesus. "Write down all you see, about the things that are, and the things that are to come."

And that's exactly what John did.

70. NEW HEAVEN, NEW EARTH!
REVELATION 21 – 22

At the end of John's vision – after the defeat of the devil and God's judgment of all people and the destruction of death and hell – there came a picture of a new beginning.

John saw a new heaven. And he saw a new earth. For the first heaven and first earth had passed away.

And then he saw a new Jerusalem, the holy city. And it was as beautiful to look at as a bride is on her wedding day – dressed to impress the one she is about to marry.

As the new Jerusalem came down from heaven, John heard a voice from God's throne.

"Look!" the voice said. "Look and see! From now on, God will live with people. They will be his people, and he will be their God!

"Tears? He will wipe them away, and every eye will be dry.
For death will be dead, and mourning just a memory.
And why would we cry when pain no longer reigns?
All of that is gone. Done. Over. Finished.
Look! Look and see! I am making everything new!"

The city shone like a precious jewel. With twelve gates for the twelve tribes of Israel and twelve foundations for the twelve apostles.

The walls were encrusted with jewels, each gate was a massive pearl, and the streets were paved with transparent gold!

There was something missing from this new Jerusalem though – something that had been right at the heart of the old Jerusalem: a temple.

And that's because there was no longer any need for one.

God himself was the temple, along with Jesus the Lamb.

And as for the sun and moon, there was no need for them either. For God's glory provided the light, and the lamp was the Lamb!

And then John saw the nations – people from every country and every land – walking by that light into the city.

(Do you remember what Isaiah said God's people would be? A light to the nations!)

But nothing wrong or false went into the city. No. Only those whose sins had been forgiven by Jesus the Lamb – whose names were found in the book of the Lamb.

Then the angel showed John even more. There was a river, clear as crystal, flowing from the throne of God and of the Lamb. And on either side of the river grew the tree of life – the special tree we first saw in the garden of Eden. Remember?

Now all of Jesus' followers could eat from that tree and live for ever. Loving Jesus as their King for ever and ever.

And Jesus, the long-promised King and Messiah, made a promise for everyone who follows him as their King…

"Yes, I am coming soon."

WHAT NEXT?

Lots of things can be your king.

For some people, money is king. For others, it's power or fame. And, just like Adam and Eve, many people make themselves king and live life according to their own rules.

But the story of the kingdom and the King demonstrates, time and time again, that making a thing other than God your king leads to sadness, emptiness, disappointment and disaster. That's what the people of Israel discovered. And that is why God came to live among them, in the person of Jesus the King, to show them a different way to live.

So, Jesus not only talked about the kingdom; he lived the kingdom life. And he showed everyone how much better it is to live their lives like that too. Everyone, including you and me!

A life dedicated to healing the hurts of the poor and the sick and the outcasts, as Jesus did when he made the sick well and ate with those whom other people had rejected.

A life of mercy and humility and peace, as Jesus demonstrated.

A life that trusts in the truth of God's word, as Jesus did when he defeated the devil's temptations.

A life marked by forgiveness, rooted in the forgiveness that Jesus won for us when he died on the cross.

And a life meant to be lived for ever, made real by Jesus' resurrection.

What do you need to do to live that life?

Tell Jesus that you want him to be your King.

Accept his forgiveness for all the wrong things you have done.

Invite his Holy Spirit to live inside you to give you the power to make his kingdom life real in your life too.

Lots of things can be your king.

But the only king that truly brings you life and love and joy is the King whose name is Jesus.

BIBLICAL | RELEVANT | ACCESSIBLE

At The Good Book Company we are dedicated to helping Christians and local churches grow. We believe that God's growth process always starts with hearing clearly what he has said to us through his timeless and flawless word—the Bible.

Ever since we opened our doors in 1991, we have been striving to produce resources that are biblical, relevant, and accessible. By God's grace, we have grown to become an international publisher, encouraging ordinary Christians of every age and stage and every background and denomination to live for Christ day by day and equipping churches to grow in their knowledge of God, their love for one another, and the effectiveness of their outreach.

Call one of our friendly team for a discussion of your needs or visit one of our local websites for more information on the resources and services we provide.

Your friends at The Good Book Company

thegoodbook.com | thegoodbook.co.uk
thegoodbook.com.au | thegoodbook.co.nz